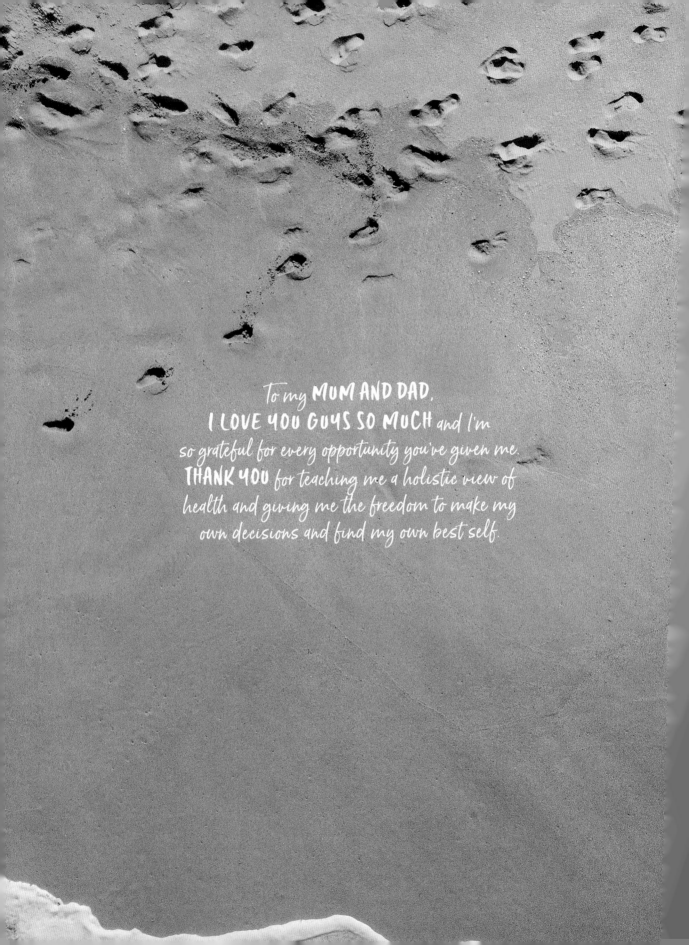

To my **MUM AND DAD,**
I LOVE YOU GUYS SO MUCH and I'm
so grateful for every opportunity you've given me.
THANK YOU for teaching me a holistic view of
health and giving me the freedom to make my
own decisions and find my own best self.

SALLY FITZGIBBONS

Summer Fit All Year Round

Pan Macmillan Australia

Contents

NOTE FROM SALLY

Hey guys,

First of all, thanks for picking up *Summer Fit*! This is my philosophy on food, health and wellness, and I can't wait to share it with you. I'll show you how I eat to nourish my body; the fuel I rely on to perform as an elite athlete; the training I do to stay in shape all year round; and how I take care of myself so that I can enjoy everything life has to offer.

I've been lucky enough to spend the past 10 years travelling the world as a professional surfer, soaking up different cultures, foods and experiences, while chasing my dream of winning a world title. I've been inspired by sporting legends, coached by experts and introduced to amazing fans, and these experiences have motivated me to do my part to bring us all closer together.

Two years ago, I started my company with the goal of connecting as many people as possible to share their health and fitness knowledge and experiences. I wanted to create a platform where we can come together and inspire each other. Energy is everywhere; it's what fuels us, drives us and brings us together.

Last year I launched my fitness app, the All Australian Beach Body; produced the world's largest female surf event, the International Beach Festival; and founded my charity, The Sally Fitzgibbons Foundation, to help combat the global childhood obesity epidemic. And we're just getting started!

Your *Summer Fit* 4-week plan is filled with my favourite recipes, workouts and advice for dialling your mindset in to achieving your goals. Spoiler alert: the secret lies in your daily routine, and I hope you'll find lots of tips for making your health and wellbeing a priority, not a chore. The recipes and information in these pages will guide you to make healthy choices in and out of the kitchen, give you fresh insights into the power of quality nutrition, and help you understand which foods are best for you. And, of course, I want to show you just how delicious nutritious food can be!

Enjoy!

Keep smiling
SALLY x

ABOUT ME

HITTING THE GROUND RUNNING

Ocean. Adventure. Energy. My childhood was made of simple ingredients, but it was perfect. Growing up in a tiny town in New South Wales called Gerroa, our back lawn stretched from the veranda across the headland all the way to the sand, where it met our playground: the ocean.

I had three older brothers and I wanted to do everything they could. Whether it was surfing waves, bike-riding, playing cricket in the backyard or wrestling in the lounge room, I had a real stubbornness that meant no matter how hard my brothers pinched or kicked or Chinese-burned me, I wouldn't stop chasing them – even trying to beat them!

We were a country family, on a budget, so the food we ate had to come in bulk and work for everyone.

We'd run home from the beach and order off Mum's 'egg menu' – scrambled, soft-boiled with soldiers, French toast, all the classics. Even then, I appreciated the value of how well she'd fuel us up. And now, wherever I am in the world, eating a soft-boiled egg takes me straight back to her kitchen. Food memories are powerful like that.

When looking at my lifestyle as an athlete, it's easy for people to forget that I grew up on the diet of a typical Aussie kid! I ate a Vegemite and cheese sandwich almost every day from kindergarten to Year 11. Mum always had nutritious food on the table at mealtimes, but we were allowed all the normal treats: Maccas pit stops on trips up the coast, Nutella sandwiches with milkshakes, even hot-chip sandwiches with chicken salt once a week!

My competitive nature emerged with my brothers, and then it grew. It was completely ingrained in me to want to be the best: I'd wake up before sunrise to squeeze in as much as possible before going to school. I'd run a few blocks of Gerroa, come home and then get into some boxing in the garage, just like Rocky, followed by crunches, push-ups and a bit of skipping.

As the sun rose I would sprint into the water for a morning surf, pretending I was Layne Beachley chasing a world title. In the afternoons, before soccer, touch football or swimming practice, I'd do my running training. Our house was about 5 km from the school gates. When the final school bell rang, I'd bolt out of class, run through the playground and head to the bus. But instead of scrambling for a place, I'd just hurl my school bag on to a seat, and then the race was on – I had to beat the bus to my stop, or I was going home without my bag.

By the age of 12, I was travelling every week for soccer tournaments, touch-footy matches, running meets and surf competitions. At first it was within Australia, then the international travel kicked in. I was in sensory overload, experiencing all those strange languages, different customs, new foods and unusual flavours.

My first surf trip to Indonesia was at the age of 14, with Steph Gilmore (then 17), who's now a six-time world champion, and Tyler Wright (then 13), the 2016 world champion. On our way home to Australia we had a stopover in Padang, so the crew took us to their favourite restaurant for a bite to eat. A few hours later, my stomach started to twist into a million knots. I started throwing up, so a nurse was called and she gave me medication. Though the team did their absolute best to get me onto the plane, my food poisoning was obvious to the airline staff and I was kicked off the plane, unable to fly until I was better. I had to wait four days in Jakarta to be well enough to travel. That experience was a defining moment for me. For the first time, I started taking notice of how different foods made me feel, and started thinking about what my food philosophy would be.

Fun fact: I was a regional chess champion! It has served me well in the strategy of competitive surfing, as well as in life.

FINDING MY ELEMENT

I've always embraced hard work because I can visualise where it's taking me. In high school, the results started coming: soccer, footy, surfing, schoolwork and even *playing chess!* This only fired me up even more and I wanted to achieve in everything I did.

The only problem was, I wanted to commit 100 per cent to all my sports: soccer, running and surfing. But this just wasn't possible. Team sports were the first to go because I missed too many practices travelling to other competitions. In 2007, I ran the 800 metres and 1500 metres at the Youth Olympics, and won gold in both. Standing on that podium was my taste of Olympic glory, the most incredible feeling. Those early starts, the pure focus, the things I'd given up to reach that goal: they were all worth it.

Though I still wasn't ready to choose between running and surfing, ultimately, I had to – and in many ways, surfing chose me. At the age of 17, I scored my first perfect 10 in the final of the Surfing World Junior Champs at Narrabeen, Sydney. That score, and the victory that came after it, confirmed my choice. I went straight into the international Qualifying Series in 2008 and became the youngest person ever to qualify for the World Surf League (WSL) world tour, progressing in record time.

Plus, I'd caught the travel bug – the good kind! I started to crave the adventure that came with exploring new places.

Everywhere I go,
THE OCEAN
is my constant home.
It CHALLENGES me,
SCARES me, CLEANSES me
and CALMS me.

PUZZLE PIECES

When I was 18, I injured my back, and I couldn't run or do any gym training. Plus, my body also decided it was a good time to grow in every which way.

Despite years of training, the weight had crept on so quickly and I was freaking out. I felt lonely and isolated. I was frustrated, angry and tearful at the smallest things. I was putting so much pressure on myself. Out of desperation I tried all the celebrity diets, even the lemon detox one. It left me tired and dizzy, making matters even worse. Getting back in shape seemed an impossible task. Movement was what kept me going when I didn't feel my best. The buzz after pushing through a hard training session is the best reminder to myself of what I'm capable of. And over time, by listening to my body rather than the latest diet craze, I was able to get my body back to how it should be.

It wasn't the first or last time I've had to recalibrate my diet. Around the same time, I discovered that I'm lactose intolerant. I'd suffered from stomach aches for years. I felt heavy, tired, bloated and sometimes really sick. It wasn't until I had the tests done that I realised it was my diet causing the symptoms. Sure, it's hard sometimes, but it's worth it to be healthy on the inside.

I love to be creative in the kitchen, but I also like the simplicity of whole foods. That's why I love fruit and veggies. They contain so much flavour and texture already, you don't have to do much to create a really satisfying meal. Everywhere I travel, I love wandering around the local food markets. It's about building the best possible meal you can with what you have around you. We often stay in apartments where we have our own kitchen, because I love preparing my own food – feeling the textures, smelling fresh herbs and spices, chopping it all up. It's a really soothing experience for me.

> Mealtimes for me are really important parts of the day, where I consciously stop and savour both the food and the people I'm sharing it with.

Mealtimes for me are really important parts of the day, where I consciously stop and savour both the food and the people I'm sharing it with. When I prepare a big meal, it's usually at dinnertime, after a day packed with training, when I'm ready to wind down and enjoy time with my friends and family. During the day, I prefer to graze on nutritious snacks. When I'm at home, I'll make a big pot of soup and leave it on the stovetop so I can grab a cupful as I head past. Or I'll snack on leftover veggies, a piece of fruit or some nuts. Whatever I'm eating, I'm always mindful of putting the best fuel I can into my body to get the best out of it.

FUEL TO THE FIRE

There are so many uncontrollable elements in elite surfing. You're not just competing against your opponent, you're against the ocean. That's what I love about it. I'm always having the most fun when I'm challenged and pushing my body to the limit. And there isn't a place on earth that challenges me more than Fiji.

Tavarua is an idyllic, heart-shaped island in Fiji with pristine white sand and clear blue water. It's also home to Cloudbreak: the most dangerous, untameable, changeable wave on tour. It demands your respect. The waves are up to 10 feet high, and just a few feet underneath is an unforgiving razor-sharp reef.

Cloudbreak is aptly nicknamed Shish Kebabs!

I became well acquainted with the reef in 2012, when I first surfed Cloudbreak with my brother Si. The conditions were perfect, 6-foot waves, and Si was cheering me on as I paddled into a wave.

I rode it all the way to the inside when suddenly my board dropped out from under me and – smack! – I landed straight on the reef. Just imagine your whole body being pulled through a cheese grater. I'd taken all the impact on my wrist and had cuts all over my arm and shoulder. We headed in to see the island doctor who was confident I'd just sprained my wrist. So I paddled back out, swollen and bruised, only to fall onto the harsh reef again. Si turned to me and said, 'It's all good, Sal. I'm an electrician. I'll tape you up. Just don't tell Dad. He'll make us come home.' So he wrapped my wrist up in electrical tape! Two weeks later, when we did finally head home, I found out my wrist was broken.

Training for Cloudbreak is all about putting yourself under pressure. I do a lot of pool training and breath work, focusing on calming the mind under the pressure and oxygen deprivation. Then, at home, I'll spend hours just taking waves on the head, getting uncomfortable. We call it 'wrestling the crocodile' – literally holding your board under the water while you're being thrown around in the washing machine of white water. Then when it's time to pull the jersey on, I know that I've done everything in my power to prepare. I've done my homework, I've surfed countless hours, my equipment's all lined up. Everything's in place.

I train to be comfortable in what can quickly become a very uncomfortable scenario.

But on 1 June 2015, I was surfing round two of the Fiji Women's Pro, which is a sudden-death knockout round. The conditions were tricky and I was using all my senses to try to read them and adapt. Suddenly, the wave bottomed out and I went flying like a slingshot into the face of the wave. As I hit the water, I heard a massive CRACK. I knew something was wrong. I resurfaced, trying to grab my board, but my spatial awareness was all off. My ear was throbbing: I'd perforated my eardrum.

Fortunately, I'd already got the scores I needed to win my heat, so I could move on to round three. But the medical team taking care of me weren't keen on that. They were concerned that if I went under a wave, I wouldn't know how to get to the surface. Because of my distorted equilibrium, I might not know which way was up.

But I wasn't thinking about giving up. I was thinking about all the training I'd done, all those hours, the title I had to defend. So, the doctors got to work: waterproof casing, Blu Tack, tape, tape and more tape. By the time they had finished with me I could have lined up in the front row of a footy team! The rest of that day is a surreal blur of adrenaline, pushing through the pain to chase my dream. I surfed all the way to the final and won. It's a special victory for me.

I think that adversity is relative. We all have challenges and battles to fight, whether they last hours, weeks, months or years. For me, the key is looking past the challenge and never losing sight of your goal. And most importantly, I've found that developing positive daily habits is the secret ingredient to success. It's all about the small efforts, day in, day out.

Positive daily habits are like putting a dollar in your savings account. Imagine every day you're investing one dollar in your happiness, your health, your fitness. Watch that build over a year, add compound interest for consistency, and you're talking about some serious health wealth! The following pages detail the daily habits that keep me happy, fit and healthy. I call these The Little Things.

THE *Little* THINGS

MORNINGS

One of the keys to making the most of my day is to get up and out there as early as possible. I think the way you spend your first few hours really determines the rest of the day. I guarantee that once you're out of bed, the hard part is over! Whatever you're planning to do with your bonus hours, have your clothes and gear right there, so you're ready to go. A morning ritual is something everyone can incorporate into their day, to bring a feeling of order, calm and harmony. It works for me. Why not give it a go?

THE EARLY BIRD

I love being up before the sun. It's the most epic headstart on the day. But I promise you, I don't wake up naturally at 4.30 am! Sometimes I need to set three alarms to make sure I wake up. But I always force myself up. I don't give myself an opportunity to think, 'What if I just stay in bed, roll over and go back to sleep?'

I'm always half asleep until I open the front door and feel the morning air on my face. But that's what I love about it. The new day is like an elixir – refreshing and healing. And there's a quiet and calmness about that time of the morning, like I've got the world to myself and the whole day ahead is just waiting for me.

I don't get up early because it's easy. It's about the commitment to myself, and the sense of reward I get from making the most of my day.

RUNNING

There are three main benefits I get from running. It's grounding, in every sense of the word. Instantly I feel connected to the day, connected to the land and connected to myself. It's my meditation, the time where I make sense of my thoughts and feelings, wins and losses, highs and lows, as I put one foot in front of the other. It leaves me feeling completely empowered to be exactly who I want to be. It's important to find your outlet, that special thing that lets your mind relax and run free, whether it's running, walking, yoga or sitting in a quiet corner. It will help you stay energised and on top of your game.

MORNING SURF

As soon as there's enough light, I'm in the water. Sometimes the sun isn't up yet, but I love that time because everyone else is still in bed. I love surfing breaks all around the world. Whenever I'm in the water, I'm home. As well as this connection with the ocean, as a surfing community we're connected on social media too. So, I can fly from Australia to France, paddle out for a surf, and someone will say to me, 'Hey Sal, the waves looked awesome in Sydney this week!'

FUEL

There is no way you can go surfing or running and not get hungry. At the end of a session, I always want to get one more wave, but I'm so pumped to head home and tuck in to an amazing breakfast. I love dreaming up what I'm going to eat while I'm still in the water. There's something about avocado on toast that's close to the heart of surfers everywhere. It's my first big meal of the day, but by the time I sit down to eat I've already worked so hard to get to that point I make sure I savour every mouthful.

Throughout the rest of the day, I'll graze on whatever's in the kitchen — a mixture of fruit, protein and leftovers. I like to keep moving through the day, so I'm always snacking to keep my energy levels topped up.

THE *Little* THINGS

DAYLIGHT HOURS

My day-to-day life is an exhilarating whirlwind of different activities. I love it. I can bounce between surfing, training, developing my fitness app, the Foundation, whatever projects we're working on. I'm still that little kid running around trying to fit as much as possible into the day! But no matter what's on the cards, there are some things that never change – whatever I am doing, these are my rituals for finding balance in my body and my mind.

TRAINING

I train in the gym most days. Or, if I'm travelling, I'll use whatever I can find – a park bench is sometimes all you need! For me, it has always been about creativity. As a kid, I used to run around at council pickup time – when everyone puts their unwanted stuff out on the kerb – and find gym equipment nobody wanted, clean it up and make it mine. So, my training's never been set around specific equipment. I love dreaming up new ways to challenge my body. I'm always focused on where I want to be. Visualisation is such an important tool.

BE YOUR OWN SENSEI

Starting my own business has been one of my most exciting adventures yet but, as you'd imagine, it has also completely changed the rhythm of my life! I bet I'm not the only one who feels like there's a constant tug of war between everything I want to do, and the downtime I need to be able to get up and do it all again tomorrow! Surrounding yourself with friends, family and colleagues who know how to support you is so important.

JOURNAL

START SOMEWHERE

Knowing when to push yourself, when to rest, and how to juggle others' expectations is a skill that takes time to master! Before putting too much pressure on yourself to do *everything, everyday,* all you need to do is say a task out loud. This might not work in every scenario, as we all have commitments we can't break, but it's a helpful tool to digest those moments when things start to get overwhelming. I've learned that energy is so much more powerful when you focus on one thing at a time. If you try and focus on everything 100 per cent of the time, you'll just get scrambled eggs.

CONSISTENCY

With travel and other commitments, it can be a squeeze to pack it all into the day. I think time is our most precious commodity. Rushing to get everything done, juggling work, deadlines, responsibilities … when you're run off your feet, it can be hard to rally the extra energy for a workout. On those days, more than ever, I like to look at my workouts not as training or exercise, but as self-care. It's one of the ways to give back to my body. Sometimes it even takes a little bit of tough love to fire up for a training session. And while you never feel awesome if you miss a session, trust me, you'll *always* feel awesome when you make time for yourself and push through those little pinch moments. And over time, as you move more and more, it becomes something your body craves.

KEEP A DIARY

I have three diaries. One's an electronic bird's eye view of where I'll be, and when. The next one is day-by-day, hard facts — who, what, where. I love switching between different parts of my life — surf, business, friends, fitness. But to do that I've got to be like a light switch, clicking from one job to another, and giving each one my undivided attention. Being organised allows me to do that without anything falling through the cracks.

My third diary is more about my connection with the ocean. It's a way to capture those feelings, remind myself of good days and bad days and articulate those experiences. I find that we're always looking for what's next. But stopping for a second to look back on what I've done is a really valuable tool. It's a way to restore some energy.

If you start a sentence out loud with "I should … ", that's a sign that there are outside elements doing the talking, pulling you in a different direction to where you know you need to be.

THE Little THINGS
EVENINGS

Everything in life needs to have balance. Day and night, rain and shine, light and shade. I've learned through experience to respect that balance in my daily routine. After a busy day, it's so important to refill the tank. I have grown to love the twilight hours, when I let my mind unwind and my body recover.

THE WIND-DOWN

At the end of the day you'll always find me hanging out on the balcony with a cup of tea, my family or a good book. I know there are a million other things I could be doing in that moment, but allowing myself to sit quietly and watch the waves and see the sun gradually slip over the horizon helps me to wind down the momentum of the day – to turn off my mind and let my body switch gears. When we tear around all day, we're often running on adrenaline, which triggers our 'fight or flight' response. Our bodies are rushing to keep up with everything we're trying to do. It's not until we stop that we can begin to rest, digest, repair and restore.

TUNING IN TO YOUR BODY

Everything we do, all day, every day, requires energy. But unfortunately we don't always have an endless supply. I've learned the hard way what it's like to exhaust your adrenal glands – just imagine your car running out of fuel in the middle of a busy highway. We all have things we want to achieve, and no matter what they are, they usually come with a fair amount of stress. Recognising and coping with that stress is an important daily practice for me.

> Your adrenal glands are responsible for producing essential hormones that control your wake–sleep cycles, regulate blood pressure, and manage stress. Adrenal fatigue compromises your ability to produce these hormones and can leave you feeling extremely tired.

There are definitely going to be days when you're running on empty, and there's no way you can tackle a big training session. I feel like that some days. So, what do I do when I know I need to refuel the tank? I let my imagination kick in. I might do a yoga session in my living room, or walk down to the beach to dip my toes in the ocean. At the end of a pool session, I'll just float in the water for a few minutes. It's the most calming thing ever. It's about giving back to your body, dialling back in and connecting with yourself. Over time, you'll build up an awareness and instinctively know where you're at, and what you need.

DINNER

Cooking for me is a lot like training – it's an adventure, an experiment. I'm not a professional cook, and when you're trying to fit as much as you can into the day, spending hours in the kitchen isn't practical, but I always take the time to prepare my own simple dishes at dinnertime. First, I choose what protein my body's craving. It could be fish, it might be red meat, or maybe chicken. I love watching cooking shows and reading through food books to get ideas. From there, I'll grab the ingredients, and then just follow my nose.

EVENING STRETCH

Wherever I go in the world, my fit ball comes with me. And every night before bed, I take half an hour to stretch out and realign, head to toe. Sure, as an athlete, it's important for me to be tuned in to every inch of every muscle. But any repetitive movement – whether it's surfing, running, sitting at a desk or just looking down at our phones – puts pressure on our joints and muscles. Tuning in to my body each evening allows me to stay on top of any niggles. With any tension or strain in the body, prevention is so much easier than cure.

The
POWER
of FOOD

I wrote this book in the hope that the information in these pages, and the recipes that follow, will inspire you to add more fruit and veg to your plate. When we choose wholefoods over processed foods, we are setting ourselves up for good health by packing our bodies full of vitamins, minerals, nutrients, antioxidants and fibre. This leads to increased energy levels, a healthier and more sustainable weight and better brain function. What's not to love?

EAT A RAINBOW

My approach to meals is what I like to call 'meat and creative three veg'. I love dreaming up new combinations and filling up my plate with an assortment of colours and flavours. Not only does it keep things interesting, but we also gain a variety of nutrients from different-coloured foods. And that's the key to a healthy diet – consuming a balanced and varied range of foods, incorporating at least five portions of vegetables and two portions of fruit a day.

While we're accustomed to meat or starchy carbs being the hero of our meals, with a bit of luck you'll find some new hero ingredients on the following pages. I'll show you the nutritional benefits of eating a wide range of fruit and vegetables in every colour of the rainbow – red, pink, orange, yellow, green, blue and purple!

Australian dietary guidelines from the National Health and Medical Research Council recommend that adults between the ages of 19 and 50 should be eating 18–20 different types of food across the five core food groups **every day** to maintain a balanced diet. However, research shows that most Aussies are averaging only 17 a week! This means that many of us are missing out on the health benefits of a whole range of foods.

Here are my top tips to add more variety to your diet:

- **Choose veggie-laden snacks** such as veggie juices and smoothies and veggie muffins or frittatas. Or just snack on raw veggie sticks.

- **Up your fruit intake** to two servings a day by making delicious smoothies for breakfast or snacks. I also love adding fruit to my salads for a natural hit of juicy goodness!

- **Mix legumes** into your curries, pasta sauces and salads.

- **Make sure your bread is always multigrain** for maximum fibre content.

- **Be conscious of what you're eating** – set yourself a challenge and track how you've done by keeping a food diary.

RED/PINK

Red fruits and vegetables are rich in lycopene and anthocyanins. Lycopene is a powerful antioxidant responsible for giving many fruit and vegetables (especially tomatoes) their red colour. Antioxidants protect the body from damage by free radicals (harmful molecules), which can be a factor in the development of cardiovascular disease and cancer. Anthocyanin is another antioxidant found in deep-red fruit and vegetables, and has been linked with numerous health benefits including improved cardiovascular health and cancer prevention. The ellagic acid in strawberries, raspberries and pomegranates has also been linked to cancer prevention. These red fruits are high in vitamin C, which can be beneficial for fighting off colds and flu.

Cherries

Strawberries

Raspberries

Pink grapefruit

Blood oranges

Pomegranate

Watermelon

Tomatoes

Red capsicum

Beetroot

Chilli

Chilli is a great source of vitamin C and also stimulates the release of endorphins – those wonderful feel-good hormones that are also natural painkillers!

ORANGE/YELLOW

Orange and yellow fruits and vegetables, such as pineapple, mangoes, sweet potatoes and carrots, are packed with vitamin C, vitamin A, zeaxanthin, flavonoids, lycopene and potassium. These foods have also been linked to reduced blood pressure, a reduced risk of prostate cancer and the promotion of healthy joints and bones, and are thought to boost the immune system. Citrus fruits contain antioxidants that work to reduce inflammation and prevent chronic disease.

Sweet potatoes

Mangoes

Mandarins

Carrots

Carrots contain vitamin A, which aids eye health, and that's just the start!

Oranges

Lemons

Lemons are rich in antioxidants with antibacterial properties, which boosts our immunity and helps us fight colds and flu.

Bananas

Pineapple

Corn

Corn is a great source of vitamins, fibre and folate.

GREEN

Green foods like broccoli, beans, avocado and pears contain nutrients such as folate, calcium and vitamin C. They're also rich in fibre, which helps keep you regular with normal bowel movements. Choosing green vegetables over other, higher-calorie foods can assist in reducing overall calorie intake, which can help with weight loss. Loading up your plate with greens can aid in reducing cholesterol levels and boosting the immune system. Be sure to include both raw and cooked greens (try spinach, kale and other dark leafy greens) in your diet, as heat can destroy some of the vitamins present.

Dark leafy greens

Spinach, kale and other dark leafy greens are full of antioxidants and phytonutrients, which are important for eye health and fighting disease. Research suggests that they may also protect us from UV radiation.

Lettuce

Avocado

Avocados are my favourite thing to add to just about any meal! They provide antioxidants and healthy fats, which have been shown to reduce inflammation.

Broccoli

Baby spinach

Pumpkin seeds

Pumpkin seeds are a great addition to a salad – just 3 tablespoons contain nearly half the recommended daily dose of magnesium.

Alfalfa sprouts

Alfalfa sprouts pack a big nutritional punch into a tiny package! They have concentrated levels of vitamins K and C, and calcium.

Beans

Kiwi fruit

Kiwi fruits are a particularly awesome source of vitamins that promote healthy bones, skin and eyes. Plus, they contains an enzyme that helps with digestion and absorption of important nutrients.

Brussels sprouts

Brussels sprouts provide us with a good hit of vitamin C!

Peas

Pears

BLUE/PURPLE

Blue and purple foods – such as eggplant, purple cabbage, plums and blueberries – contain many different nutrients, some of which are also found in red/pink fruit and vegetables. These include lutein, flavonoids, vitamin C and ellagic acid, which help the body absorb calcium, support healthy digestion and help fight inflammation. The antioxidant anthocyanin, also present in blue/purple foods, has been linked with numerous health benefits including improved cardiovascular health and cancer prevention.

Blackberries

The fibre and vitamin A in blackberries help us to maintain a healthy digestive system.

Blueberries

Blueberries are the poster children for antioxidants! These little gems help the body fight free radicals and keep our brains sharp. Research suggests they may also help prevent Alzheimer's disease and dementia.

Figs

Figs are one of my favourite foods, and they've been used in nutritional therapy for centuries! An excellent source of fibre, figs are packed with calcium, especially when dried, and also contain potassium, magnesium, iron and vitamins A, E and K.

Purple cabbage

Eggplant

Beetroot

Beetroot are incredible purple-power foods that support our bones and muscles thanks to their calcium and magnesium content. They're also anti-inflammatory!

Plums

Natural
PICK-ME-UPS

Nature can provide some amazing remedies when we're feeling under the weather. Try these natural foods to boost your energy levels and shorten your downtime, so you can get back to enjoying life again!

COLDS AND FLU

We need zinc for the development and function of particular immune cells that can prevent colds and flu. The best food sources are oysters, pumpkin seeds, almonds, walnuts, buckwheat, turkey and chicken.

Vitamin C is also excellent for the proper function of our immune system, so look for foods such as berries, lemon, grapefruit, oranges, red capsicum and green leafy veggies, such as kale, broccoli, brussels sprouts and cabbage.

When suffering from a cold or flu, staying hydrated is essential. Aim to drink at least eight glasses of water a day.

A hot lemon and honey tea made with manuka or raw honey before bed can help to relieve night-time coughing.

Chicken soup as a cold treatment is not just an old wives' tale – it has been found to have a mild anti-inflammatory effect that helps to clear mucus!

NAUSEA AND VOMITING

When suffering from nausea or vomiting, staying hydrated is again really important. Increase your water intake, or suck on ice cubes if you're struggling to keep fluids down. When you can eat, aim to get as broad a range of nutrients as possible from multiple food groups.

Ginger and peppermint have anti-nausea properties, so try boiling some water and make a tea out of fresh ginger and peppermint. When you're eating again, simple foods may be easier to start with, such as bread, rice, potatoes, lean meat and bananas.

Did you know ginger is a natural antibiotic that helps our bodies to detoxify, reduce congestion and stimulate circulation? Ginger and garlic both have excellent immune-boosting properties, so try adding these to your meals whenever you can (raw is best).

THAT TIME OF THE MONTH

The best way to combat PMS is to adopt a completely wholefood diet, free from sugar, refined carbohydrates, caffeine, processed food and alcohol. Removing these foods can help to balance your hormones and, in turn, reduce your symptoms. After making this change, if you still suffer from PMS, make sure you include plenty of calcium in your diet (in the form of almonds, sesame seeds, green leafy vegetables and dairy).

Vitamin D is involved in hormone production and is also required for the absorption of calcium, so it's important to ensure you get enough. The best source is sunshine, but eggs, green leafy vegetables and fish will also top up your vitamin-D levels.

Magnesium is also involved in the absorption of calcium and helps to relax our muscles and ease cramping. Sources include dark chocolate, green leafy vegetables, almonds, cashews, brown rice, oats and legumes.

Phytoestrogens are compounds that have a balancing effect with oestrogen (PMS can often be a result of excess oestrogen), so look for foods containing these, such as miso, tempeh, chickpeas, buckwheat, quinoa, barley, oats, linseeds, sesame seeds, sunflower seeds, pumpkin seeds, lentils and kidney beans.

FOOD-PREP HACKS

One of the biggest challenges to eating well is finding the time to prepare and cook great meals. Rushing around can lead to poor last-minute decisions about food, and a quick fix is rarely as healthy as we'd like it to be!

Here are my tips for dealing with these panic moments:

1. **Plan your grocery shopping in advance** – put time into planning the meals you'll be eating for the week and buy everything in one go to avoid the excuses of missing ingredients or having to make an extra trip to the shops. Use your freezer if you need to ensure that any fresh ingredients don't spoil.

2. **Buy some extra veggies in your weekly shop to enjoy as sides or snacks.** Carrot sticks, celery and sliced capsicum are all great options. Dip them in a nut butter or hummus for a little protein hit to keep you powering through your day.

3. **When shopping for greens,** choose ones that are not showing any signs of wilting or damage and have no areas turning yellow or brown.

4. **Keep your favourite chopped veggies in the freezer, ready to toss into any meal to boost the nutrient value.** Frozen veg is actually still very nutritious and can sometimes be a better option than a product that has travelled many food miles to reach your kitchen.

5. **Prepare muesli, soaked oats and chia puddings in bulk on a Sunday afternoon.** They'll keep for days and are perfect for a week's worth of breakfasts.

6. **Cook grains and legumes** such as quinoa or rice in bulk – they'll keep in the fridge for three to four days and will really speed up your meal prep.

7. **Make extra servings of salads,** but keep the dressing on the side. Store in an airtight container, then all you need to do is add protein, drizzle over the dressing and you're all set!

8. **Have ready-to-eat protein sources stocked up.** Try canned fish, legumes and boiled eggs.

9. **Create smoothies in advance to freeze.** Just pop all the solid ingredients into a freezer bag and freeze. When required, add the ingredients to your blender with the liquid component. Perfect for breakfasts or snacks!

ORGANIC AND SEASONAL
WHOLEFOODS

The fuel you put in the tank is so important. To get the best out of your body and enjoy life, treat yourself to the most natural and delicious foods you can. Choosing wholefoods over processed foods, incorporating a wide range of seasonal fruits and veggies into your diet, and buying organic when available are all good investments in your health and wellbeing.

PROCESSED FOODS VERSUS WHOLEFOODS

Need any more evidence that natural wholefoods are best for our bodies? Perhaps it's worth a look at what's *not* in wholefoods, and what you'll find in processed alternatives. Foods that have been altered from their natural state are often made from refined ingredients and artificial substances. They are usually:

- **High in sugar** – excessive sugar can have adverse effects on your metabolism, insulin resistance and levels of 'bad' cholesterol.

- **Sweet, salty or fatty** – the more of these foods we have, the more our tastebuds begin to favour these flavour profiles and these foods then become addictive.

- **Full of artificial ingredients** – which aren't food!

- **High in refined carbs and low in nutrients** – which leads to blood-sugar spikes and nutritional deficiencies.

GOING ORGANIC

Organic food is a great choice, but it's not affordable for everyone, and when I'm travelling I don't always have the luxury of organic options. I always wash and scrub all of my fruit and vegetables well to remove as many toxins as possible. Pesticides actually accumulate in fatty areas, so if you have a budget for organic food, use it on your meats, nuts, seeds, oils and dairy first.

EATING BY THE SEASON

We're so lucky in Australia to have easy access to a wide variety of amazing fresh produce all year round. Whether I'm at home or travelling for competitions, I always make sure I'm eating seasonally. There are so many reasons to do so! Food in season tastes better, contains more nutrients, is cheaper and helps save the planet in terms of fewer food miles and needing less pesticides and modification to grow.

In summer, there's nothing I love more than sitting out on the balcony after a surf with some friends, a watermelon and a few spoons! But in winter I get out the slow cooker in the morning and throw in some meat and veg to simmer all day and fill the house with the smell of comfort food. Embracing seasonal tastes, textures and cooking methods is nourishing for your mind and your body.

Plate
REAL ESTATE

At mealtimes, your plate should be made up of 25 per cent low-GI (glycaemic index) carbohydrates, 25 per cent lean protein and 50 per cent non-starchy veggies. There should be a small amount (1–2 tablespoons) of healthy fats per meal. These four food groups are essential to good health and nutrition.

25%
Low-GI carbohydrates

50%
Non-starchy veggies

25%
Lean protein

Healthy fats

Carbohydrates are the fuel source for many vital organs, including the brain, kidneys and central nervous system, so it is important not to cut these out! GI relates to the time it takes for foods to break down and the effect this has on blood-glucose levels. Foods that have a low GI are best, as they release glucose slowly, giving us sustained energy rather than peaks and troughs. Good examples of low-GI foods are grainy bread, pasta, oats, brown rice and sweet potato.

Protein builds, maintains and replaces muscle and tissue. It's also important for the production of enzymes, hormones and neurotransmitters. Protein is made up of amino acids and there's a certain number of amino acids that are referred to as 'essential', meaning we cannot make them ourselves and must source them from our diet. Protein-rich foods include eggs, chicken, red meat, seafood, legumes, soy and quinoa. Shop mindfully when buying your meat, fish and other protein sources: each serve should be approximately the size of the palm of your hand.

Non-starchy vegetables are full of fibre, and are high in vitamins and minerals. Non-starchy vegetables are lower in calories than starchy ones and include all of our coloured vegetables except for potato, sweet potato, corn and parsnips (which are classified as starchy).

YOUR INNER CHAMPION

It's important to find the right balance of fuel and energy that allows your body to thrive.

HOW MUCH SHOULD I EAT?

There's no 'one size fits all' approach when it comes to how much we should be eating. Our age, gender, life stage, height and level of physical activity all need to be considered when working out how much to eat. To find what's best for you, start with three well-balanced meals and two snacks per day and take note of how you feel. If you find your energy levels are too low, or you're super-active, you might need to eat more. If you find yourself feeling sleepy after a big meal, you might like to try smaller meals eaten more frequently throughout the day.

You hold the key to find your own inner champion and, in the following pages, I give you the information to navigate all aspects of eating with balance and mindfulness.

I love having a nourishing breakfast after a morning full of training, and after that I prefer to snack on smaller meals every few hours to keep my energy levels topped up without losing momentum. But everyone's different and should eat according to their own preferences, lifestyle and needs. If you're unsure, consider consulting a nutritionist or dietician to help you work out the healthiest and most suitable approach for you.

DEALING WITH INTOLERANCES

Food intolerances cause symptoms such as bloating and digestive issues, because the body is unable to process certain foods. Food allergies cause an immune-system reaction, which can be severe. Symptoms include rashes and swelling, which can be life-threatening. If you think you might be intolerant or allergic to certain foods, it's important to seek professional advice. Here are the most common intolerances and advice on when to seek help.

Dairy/lactose intolerance

Symptoms – bloating, diarrhoea, gas, abdominal pain.

Don't immediately cut all dairy from your diet if you suspect you are lactose intolerant, as you'll miss out on a number of essential nutrients. Try cutting down your dairy intake or focusing on hard cheeses, cream, butter and cottage cheese, which contain little or no lactose, to see if this improves your symptoms.

When to see a medical professional – if reducing your intake of dairy does not change your symptoms, see a GP or nutritionist who may diagnose you via a hydrogen breath test and/or an elimination diet.

If dairy elimination is recommended, it is important that you source calcium from other foods such as sardines, salmon, soy, almonds, sesame seeds, seaweed, leafy greens, hazelnuts, parsley, sunflower seeds, black beans and quinoa. Vitamin D and magnesium are also important to help the absorption of calcium (see page 35 for dietary sources).

Wheat/gluten intolerance

Symptoms – gas, bloating, diarrhoea, constipation, headaches, swelling, mood issues, fatigue.

The only way to combat a gluten intolerance is to eliminate gluten from your diet completely. Gluten-containing grains include wheat (and wheat varieties including spelt), barley, oats, rye, triticale, malt (in all forms) and brewer's yeast. The good news is that there are plenty of gluten-free grains to choose from, including rice, quinoa, amaranth, millet and buckwheat.

When to see a medical professional – if you think you may have a gluten intolerance it's important to see a health professional and have a blood or skin-prick test to rule out coeliac disease, as this can lead to severe health complications.

Nut allergies

Symptoms – tingling mouth and lips, swelling of the face, nausea, hives, throat tightness, difficulty breathing, fast heart rate.

If you experience these symptoms, avoid nuts and all nut products (including oils, butters and foods that have traces of nuts). You should ensure you eat a balanced diet with plenty of meat, chicken, fish, vegetables, wholegrains, legumes and fruit to cover your nutritional requirements.

When to see a medical professional – if you experience symptoms after eating nuts, see a GP who may test for allergies using a skin-prick test, blood test or elimination diet. Once an allergic reaction has occurred it's important to get treatment as soon as possible. Mild reactions should be treated with an antihistamine; severe (anaphylactic) reactions must be treated with an adrenaline pen and an ambulance should be called immediately. The reaction may require oxygen, steroids and antihistamines in the ambulance or in hospital.

NAVIGATING TRENDS

For medically diagnosed food intolerances and allergies, it's essential to modify your diet to either reduce or completely eliminate these food groups. For everyone else, there is no need to reduce or eliminate these foods from your diet, even if the supermarkets are filling their shelves with gluten-free products and magazines are full of your favourite celebrities who swear their recent weight-loss is due to giving up dairy.

Giving up any food group may lead to short-term weight-loss if you reduce your overall intake of food, but in the long run we often end up replacing these wholefoods with more processed alternatives, which lack nutrients. The ongoing impact of missing out on the essential nutrients and minerals found in whole food groups has a detrimental effect on your overall health and wellbeing.

Keep your diet balanced and varied, and don't make extreme choices unless you need to for medical reasons.

SUPPLEMENTS AND PROTEIN POWDERS

If you're eating a well-balanced diet filled with a range of different wholefoods, then supplements shouldn't be necessary. However, additional challenges and health concerns – such as training for a marathon, suffering chronic stress or dealing with long-term illness – can increase our nutritional requirements. Be sure to seek out natural options and speak to a GP or nutritionist for recommendations of reputable brands.

Protein powder is one supplement that can be beneficial in smoothies for post-workout snacks. Make sure you go for a product that is as natural as possible. Check the ingredients lists before purchasing to make sure it's short and doesn't contain many (if any) artificial flavours, colourings or sweeteners. Go for a reputable brand recommended by a health professional and don't get drawn in by fancy packaging or marketing – it's all about what's in the packet, not on the packet!

HYDRATION

Water is essential for our survival. I'm surrounded by it all day, every day, and I'm always conscious of how much water my body needs! Our bodies are made of about 60 per cent water and need it to nourish the brain, remove waste and lubricate joints. The traditional rule of eight glasses per day is a good general guide but, in reality, our requirements differ depending on our age and gender, the climate and our activity level.

Australian guidelines suggest that adult women require approximately 2.1 litres of fluids a day, and adult men about 2.6 litres. Keep in mind that you'll need more if the temperature is warm, if you are physically active, if you have a hot bath or go to a sauna or steam room, if you are suffering from fever, if you work in a heated environment or if you are pregnant or breastfeeding.

The best way to keep track of your hydration levels is to pay attention to your body. If you're thirsty, or your urine is dark in colour, you'll need to increase your water intake. I'm a big fan of coconut water for an occasional alternative to water. It's natural, refreshing and a great source of electrolytes. Processed fruit juices, sports drinks and alcohol are full of sugars and, for most of us, unnecessary calories.

Personally, I don't drink coffee or black tea, and I recommend drinking caffeinated drinks in moderation to avoid dehydration and stress on our adrenal glands and nervous system. I do love to unwind in the evening with a cup of herbal tea though.

A cup of herbal tea is hydrating and comforting, and can relieve nausea, bloating and insomnia.

SLEEP

Getting enough zzzs is one of the most important, yet easily forgotten, pieces of the wellness puzzle. When we are sleeping, our bodies are working hard to repair, restore, recover and recharge. Even though we might feel like we can function with six, five or maybe even four hours' sleep, our bodies actually need between seven and nine hours each night.

If you struggle to get a good night's rest, the reason might be to do with your afternoon habits. Our bodies are programmed to unwind as the sun goes down and nighttime settles. Caffeine, alcohol, stress, screen time, bright lights and loud noises all disrupt this natural rhythm.

To improve the quality of your shut-eye, avoid caffeine and alcohol, focus on winding down with the sun, read a book instead of watching TV or looking at your phone, keep your bedroom as calm and tidy as possible and allow your body to settle in for a quality night's sleep.

MEASURE YOUR PROGRESS

Tracking every calorie and macronutrient we consume isn't necessary, but there's real value in reflecting on what you've eaten and how it's made you feel, and noting the progress you've made in your health and wellbeing journey.

Try keeping a food diary for a week or two to record how certain foods affect your wellbeing, sleep and ability to exercise. You should start to see some trends that can help you adapt your meal plan to better suit your personal needs.

For tracking physical progress, I recommend using photos. For an accurate reflection of how your body is changing, take your photos at the same time of day (morning is best), ideally on the same day of the week, in the same place, with the same lighting. Wear snug but not body-shaping clothes (like spandex tights!) or, ideally, take photos in your swimmers.

As your body transforms through changes in your diet and exercise routine, the scales may not move as much as you want, or even at all! Don't fret – you're setting the foundations for a healthier, happier and stronger you that will be sustainable for years to come! Rather than setting a goal of a specific weight, pay attention to how certain items of clothes are fitting. Focus on reaching a point where you have a balanced diet you can maintain, and where you feel happy and healthy within your body.

A number on a scale does not determine how fit, strong, happy or confident you are.

EATING OUT

Eating well at home is one thing, but eating out can be a whole new challenge. And if we're honest, it's more of a mental challenge than anything else. It's about picking out the diamonds in the rough. As you're heading to the restaurant, ask yourself, 'What's the best thing I could give my body right now? What's the worst?' And somewhere in the middle, you'll find your minimum standard.

Once you're in the restaurant, look over the menu and I bet you'll be able to pick out the bad guys. You know what I mean: deep-fried things, creamy this, cheesy that. The more you skip over those options and don't give them any attention, the more your brain gets used to it. It's all about consistency. Over time, through our decisions and actions, the mind adapts.

TIPS FOR EATING OUT

1. Never go out on an empty stomach.
2. Check the menu beforehand so you know what to expect.
3. Avoid filling up on bread before the meal has even arrived.
4. Steer clear of heavy or creamy sauces, which can be hiding sugar and all sorts of additives you'd usually avoid.
5. Ask for salad dressing on the side so that you can control the quantity you're eating.
6. Request salad or vegetables as a side instead of chips or rice.

And if you need a bit of help?
Waitstaff often know the menu inside out,
and can help you select a healthy option.

Ultimately, though, don't overstress about eating out. You deserve to relax and enjoy yourself. Remember to eat your meal slowly and try not to eat to the point where you feel over-full. Don't feel pressured into having multiple courses just because others are – only you can take responsibility for your health and wellness!

Some restaurants will have more wholesome menu items than others, but most will have something suitable on offer. Here are some healthier options to consider at some of our most popular eating-out destinations:

PUB GRUB

- Steak and salad
- Grilled fish and salad
- Salads (with added protein)

Be careful with serving sizes, as pub meals can be huge! With salads, ask for the dressing on the side.

JAPANESE

- Sushi and sashimi
- Soup
- Edamame
- Salads (with added protein)

Avoid tempura and katsu meals, as they're usually deep fried. Instead, look for grilled or steamed dishes and make sure your rice portion is moderate.

THAI

- Mixed vegetable dishes – the more colours the better!
- Stir-fries
- Thai salads (with added protein)

Avoid the curries, as they are usually made with a lot of coconut cream, which is high in saturated fat.

CHINESE

- Poached fish
- Steamed or stir-fried greens

Try to avoid dumplings, deep-fried dishes and too much rice!

ITALIAN

- Fish/steak and veggies or salad
- Entree pasta with side of salad
- Share a pizza between two or three of you with a side salad

Avoid pastas with heavy, creamy sauces and pizzas with processed meats as toppings.

A great rule of thumb when eating out, no matter where you go, is to try and pick a meal that will match what your plate would look like at home: 25 per cent low-GI carbohydrates, 25 per cent lean protein and 50 per cent non-starchy veggies. There should also be a small amount (1–2 tablespoons) of healthy fats per meal.

TRAINING AND NUTRITION

I love mixing up my workouts to keep my mind engaged and my body challenged! My All Australian Beach Body (AABB) app is all about finding new ways to move your body – it's my tried and tested trick to staying motivated, and continually improving. A mix of HIIT (High Intensity Interval Training), strength and cardio training combined with some core, balance and stretching work will provide you with a healthy and challenging exercise regimen.

Getting the right nutrition for your workouts is important but it doesn't have to be difficult! Below are some simple guidelines to provide your body with what it needs at the right time.

The main things to consider when it comes to nutrition and training are:

Sustaining your workouts – Different types of training will burn different levels of energy, but no matter what kind of training it is, we always need to make sure we have enough fuel in the tank to get the most out of our session!

Encouraging fast recovery – When we exercise, we are breaking down our muscle fibres. The amount of muscle breakdown depends on the type of training, so it's important to ensure we provide enough protein and amino acids to rebuild the muscle fibres. This will reduce delayed onset muscle soreness (DOMS) but also aid in increasing muscle mass for those looking to tone up.

Maintaining hydration – Never underestimate the importance of hydration! Research shows that even the smallest amount of dehydration can negatively affect performance, and we're not just talking exercise performance – it can affect your daily jobs and tasks too. Dehydration can lead to tiredness, fatigue and headaches, so to reduce the risk of experiencing these during training and throughout the day after your workout, keeping well hydrated is key.

Head to page 66 to try my high-intensity, equipment-free FITZ workouts!

BEFORE YOUR WORKOUT

HYDRATE

Regularly sipping water pre-workout is important to maintain hydration.

FUEL YOUR BODY

When it comes to exercise and nutrition it's important to trial what works for you, because stomach upsets are not pleasant when training or performing! A full meal two to three hours before training is a good option if you are an athlete in training for a specific event, if you have the time and if you can stomach it. This meal should include carbohydrates (brown rice, quinoa, soba noodles, sweet potato) and protein (eggs, fish, turkey, chicken, red meat, quinoa) as well as a variety of coloured vegetables.

If you prefer to eat a bigger meal before your workout, one to two hours before is the ideal time to build up your reserves. This meal should include mainly carbohydrates with a small amount of protein.

Pre-workout meals:

- Banana, Almond Butter and Berry Jam on Toast (page 165)
- Smoothies with added protein powder (e.g. page 177)
- Green Fruit Salad with Cashew Cream (page 174).

Or a small carb-rich snack:

If you prefer, a small carb-rich snack is the perfect source of energy for your workout, even if you're aiming to lose weight. This could be:

- A piece of fruit
- Toast with just berry jam (page 165)
- A half-serving of a smoothie (e.g. page 177).

For workouts over 60 minutes:

Low-GI carbs such as pasta, grainy bread, oats and starchy vegetables like sweet potato and pumpkin are ideal for longer duration workouts to give you the long-lasting energy you'll need.

AFTER YOUR WORKOUT

HYDRATE

Make sure that you drink plenty of water within 30 minutes of your workout to replace fluids. As a general guide, aim for a litre of water, more if you're training in warm temperatures. Coconut water has the added benefits of potassium and magnesium, which will restore the electrolytes that are lost through sweat.

REPLACE AND REPAIR

The optimal time to refuel after training is 30–60 minutes post-workout, as this window is when our muscles are most receptive to the nutrients we provide. Within this time, go for a meal with a 3:1 ratio of carbs (including vegetables and fruit) to protein to encourage energy replacement and muscle repair. A small amount of healthy fats (omega-3 fats) is also beneficial to help reduce any exercise-induced inflammation and a variety of veg in a rainbow of colours is important for an array of micronutrients.

Even though our muscle fibres don't break down as much in cardio training as when we do strength or resistance training, protein is still important to aid a quick recovery from any muscle soreness.

Post-workout breakfasts:

- Smoothies with added protein powder (e.g. page 177)
- Green Pesto Omelette (page 166) with sourdough
- Coconut Scrambled Eggs with Asparagus on Toast (page 173).

Post-workout lunch/dinners:

- Open Lamb Burgers with Coconut Sauce (page 286)
- Black Bean and Sweet Potato Nachos (page 266)
- Pesto Prawn Pasta (page 253)
- Creamy Chicken and Spinach Wraps (page 206)
- Baked Lemon Fish with Sweet Potato Mash and Mixed Peas (page 274)
- Barramundi with Roast Pumpkin, Asparagus and Pomegranate (page 269).

The amount of protein we need varies based on our gender, body weight and workout intensity, but as a general guide your post-workout meal should contain 20–30 grams of protein. Note that 100 grams of cooked chicken breast contains 31 grams of protein.

My
4-WEEK
Plan

IT'S IMPORTANT TO THINK ABOUT your health and happiness like a recipe. No one ingredient makes the dish complete, and if one ingredient is past its use-by date, the whole dish is going to go bad. We need to take care of all the ingredients – our food and drink, exercise and rest – because they're equally important to finding your ultimate self.

So, whether you're looking for fresh inspiration, a fine-tuning of your health habits, or a total wellness overhaul, I hope that the recipes, tips and workouts on the following pages will give you the tools you need to chase your goals.

THE NEXT FOUR WEEKS ARE ALL ABOUT ...

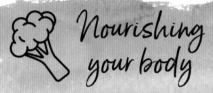

Nourishing your body

My 4-week meal plan is designed to fill your plate with a delicious variety of nourishing and tasty foods, without wasting ingredients. The carefully tailored recipes and shopping lists serve two, so you can enlist someone to enjoy them with you or halve the quantities to serve one. They're quick and easy to prepare, so you have more time to get out and enjoy life.

Finding a new fit

Each week, there are three equipment-free workouts that you can do at home, at the park or on the beach. They're high-intensity, full-body sessions, designed to get you fit, lean and strong!

Starting small

I firmly believe the path to success is about taking small, incremental steps. Let's take away the pressure of unrealistic changes, and focus on one aspect of your health each week. There are lots of little tips throughout this plan that you can pick up and try when you're ready.

Week
1.

PREP *for* SUCCESS

Are you ready to give your body the most nutritious fuel possible? Embrace that **energy** and get ahead of your goals this week by doing your shopping and some of your prep in advance. You CAN look after your health and wellness AND get the most out of life – you just need to get organised! Then you can power through the rest of your week without having to worry about finding healthy meal options.

There are three meals this week where you'll make enough for **leftovers** the next day, but you can always increase this by **cooking double** at dinnertime! And there are notes on recipes that can be made ahead of time to fast-track your mornings.

Channel your motivation into preparation.

Shopping List

21 MEALS • SERVES 2

FRESH FAVOURITES

FRUIT, VEGETABLES AND HERBS

2 green apples
2 bunches asparagus
1 avocado
1 banana
3 beetroots
½ cup (65 g) blackberries
1 cup (155 g) blueberries
1 bunch bok choy
3 heads broccoli
1 bunch broccolini
1 large butternut pumpkin
¼ red cabbage
2 red capsicums
1 yellow capsicum
4 carrots
1½ cauliflowers
2 celery stalks
2 punnets cherry tomatoes
1 long green chilli
1 small red chilli
2 long red chillies
1 corn cob
¾ cup (120 g) dried cranberries

1 Lebanese cucumber
1 packet frozen edamame
2 eggplants
1 fresh fig
11 cloves garlic
35 g ginger
½ iceberg lettuce
1 large bunch kale
3 lemons
3 limes
2 red onions
3 oranges
1 parsnip
1 pineapple
1 pomegranate
2 handfuls of rocket
3 handfuls of snowpeas
12 handfuls of baby spinach
1 bunch spring onions
2 punnets strawberries
3 zucchini
1 bunch basil
1 bunch coriander
1 bunch mint

2 sprigs rosemary
1 lemongrass stalk

MEAT, POULTRY AND SEAFOOD

200 g chicken mince
400 g chicken breast
200 g chicken tenderloins
800 g chicken thigh fillets
400 g lamb backstrap
200 g lean rump steak
200 g green (raw) prawns
200 g salmon fillet
200 g smoked salmon
200 g tuna steak (or 2 x 95 g tins)
200 g white fish fillet

I recommend buying your fish fresh on the day you are cooking it.

EGGS AND DAIRY/ALTERNATIVES

12 organic eggs
150 g goat's cheese
1 litre almond milk (or milk of your choice)
150 g coconut yoghurt (or yoghurt of your choice)

PANTRY STAPLES

GRAINS, PULSES, NUTS AND SEEDS

1 loaf sourdough bread
1½ cups (330 g) buckwheat groats
½ cup (65 g) buckwheat flour
1¾ cups (170 g) rolled oats
250 g wholegrain pasta
1 cup white quinoa
1 packet soba noodles
1 packet vermicelli noodles
1 x 400 g tin chickpeas
1 x 400 g tin brown lentils
1 cup (100 g) almond meal
¾ cup (120 g) raw almonds
¾ cup (120 g) chia seeds
1 tablespoon desiccated coconut

3 tablespoons (40 g) hazelnuts
3 tablespoons (40 g) pine nuts
1¾ cups (270 g) pumpkin seeds
½ cup (75 g) sesame seeds
1¼ cup (150 g) walnuts

SPICES, OILS AND CONDIMENTS

baking powder
bicarbonate of soda
chilli flakes
flaked coconut
ground cinnamon
ground cumin
ground nutmeg
dried oregano

ground turmeric
paprika
almond butter
apple cider vinegar
balsamic vinegar
coconut oil
coconut sugar
dijon mustard
extra virgin olive oil
fish sauce
honey
maple syrup
mirin
miso paste (light/shiro)
psyllium husk
tahini (hulled)
tamari or soy sauce

Remember to check your pantry before shopping for these ingredients. You may already have some of these things!

Monday

BREAKFAST

Banana and Fig Salted
Caramel Smoothie

PAGE 129

LUNCH

Chicken, Avocado and
Blueberry Salad

PAGE 193

DINNER

Soy, Orange and Sesame
Salmon with Greens
and Soba

PAGE 241

*You can make Tuesday's
Orange and Almond
Chia Pudding tonight
to save you time
in the morning.*

1.

Tuesday

BREAKFAST

Orange and Almond Chia Pudding

PAGE 130

The leftover half apple is perfect for a snack with a little bit of almond butter on top.

LUNCH

Pesto Tuna Salad

PAGE 194

You can make this ahead of time and just stir through the pesto before serving.

DINNER

Marinated Lamb with Roast Beet Salad

PAGE 242

SAVE LEFTOVERS for WED LUNCH

Turn your goals into plans

Regularly writing in a journal is one of my favourite ways to plan and measure success. (Read more about it on page 45.) Use this space to write down your goal for the next four weeks, and a daily action or ritual that will help you get there. Your goals can be inspired by The Little Things (on pages 16–21).

GOAL: ....

PLAN: ....

....

....

....

Wednesday

BREAKFAST

Smoked Salmon and Corn Salsa on Sourdough

PAGE 133

LUNCH

Marinated Lamb with Roast Beet Salad

PAGE 242

USE LEFTOVERS *from* TUE DINNER

DINNER

Fish Skewers with Buckwheat and Pineapple Salsa

PAGE 245

Week 1.

Thursday

BREAKFAST

Bangin' Berry Smoothie

PAGE 134

LUNCH

Quinoa with Sesame
Soft-Boiled Eggs

PAGE 197

DINNER

Oregano and Lemon
Chicken with Grilled Veggies

PAGE 246

SAVE LEFTOVERS for FRI LUNCH

Celebrate the small wins

Results are achieved over time, not overnight. But that should not stop you celebrating the small wins along the way! Give yourself a high five and write down something that you've done this week to get you closer to your goals.

BRAG ZONE:
....
....
....
....

Friday

BREAKFAST

Grilled Pineapple with Coconut Yoghurt and Mint

PAGE 137

You can swap pineapple for kiwi fruit in winter.

LUNCH

Oregano and Lemon Chicken with Grilled Veggies

PAGE 246

USE LEFTOVERS *from* THU DINNER

DINNER

Beef with Cauliflower Puree, Hazelnuts and Pomegranate

PAGE 249

Week

1.

Saturday

Weekend roast cook-ups are one of my favourite ways to prep!

BREAKFAST

Pumpkin and Cranberry Loaf

PAGE 138

LUNCH

Roasted Veggie Salad with Crunchy Chickpeas

PAGE 198

DINNER

Thai Chicken Lettuce Cups

PAGE 250

Motivation momentum

Now that you've spent a week focused on daily rituals that will get you closer to your goals, take some time at the end of the week to plan ahead and keep that momentum up. Is there another ritual you can add into the mix? Write it down here.

GOAL: ....

....

RITUAL: ....

....

....

Sunday

BREAKFAST

Broccoli and Pesto Frittata with Spiced Carrot and Orange Juice

PAGE 141

SAVE LEFTOVERS for **MON BREAKFAST**

LUNCH

Buckwheat, Strawberry and Basil Salad

PAGE 201

SAVE LEFTOVERS for **MON LUNCH**

DINNER

Pesto Prawn Pasta

PAGE 253

Whip up the Homemade Muesli for Tuesday's smoothie bowl in advance. Store in an airtight container for later.

My *FITZ* workouts!

In this 4-week plan you've got three high-intensity workouts per week – Lower Body, Upper Body and Full Body. Remember to warm up and warm down in every workout.

WARM UP

Before every workout complete the 3-minute warm-up sequence opposite. It's a time-efficient way to mobilise your joints and fire up your body. **Lunges with Thoracic Twists** open up your hips and mobilise your thoracic spine. **4pt Fast Feet** focuses on agility. You'll feel your body get nice and warm as you jump. In your **Bear Crawl**, focus on slow, controlled movements, activating your core and shoulders. Start with nice slow **Arm Rotations** then build up momentum as you feel your shoulders loosen up.

LOWER BODY

These workouts have three sets of exercises and we'll repeat each set three times for a certain duration. Take a 1-minute rest between each set and make sure you stay hydrated. Focus on proper technique as it will keep you injury-free and work all the right muscle groups.

UPPER BODY

Follow the same format as your Lower-body sessions: three sets, three repeats each, 1-minute rest between each set. As you move through the plan, we'll repeat some exercises to help muscles grow fitter and leaner – but you'll also find new challenging exercises to keep it interesting.

FULL BODY

Your Full-body workouts will be a three-set skipping pyramid. In each set, you'll alternate between a resistance exercise and skipping – increasing your reps to the top of the pyramid, then decreasing reps to come back down. If you don't have a skipping rope, get your heart rate going by skipping on the spot, doing high knees, fast feet, stair runs or beach sprints!

WARM DOWN

It's extremely important to warm down after every workout. Take my favourite stretch sequence opposite nice and slow, breathe and let your body relax. Your shoulders want to stay on the ground in your **Glute Pretzel Stretch**, and your top foot should be flexed to protect your knee. The **Lying Glute Lower-back Stretch** is an awesome twist for your spine, but don't force it. Keep your hips level in your **Hamstring Stretch**, rather than twisting. **Child's Pose** is your time to breathe deep and feel your heart rate slow down. Keep your elbow level with your shoulder in the **Wall Pec Stretch**; depending on how mobile you are, you might be able to turn your chest away from the wall to deepen the stretch.

LUNGES WITH THORACIC TWIST
30 seconds each side

4PT FAST FEET
30 seconds

Forwards and backwards!

BEAR CRAWL
30 seconds

ARM ROTATIONS
30 seconds each direction

GLUTE PRETZEL STRETCH
30 seconds each side

LYING GLUTE LOWER-BACK STRETCH
30 seconds each side

HAMSTRING STRETCH
30 seconds each side

Breathe deeply

CHILD'S POSE
60 seconds

WALL PEC STRETCH
30 seconds each side

Week

1.

Lower Body

Do as many repetitions as you can, while keeping proper form and intensity, in the allocated time. In your **Wide Squats,** keep your feet at least hip-width apart, your chest nice and tall, and turn your toes out slightly. Make sure you can feel your glutes activating! When you take this into a **Squat Jump,** focus on an explosive movement and landing light on your toes. If you feel any pain in your knees, stick to normal squats.

Reverse Lunges are all about alignment. Keep your knees in line with your toes, not pointing in or out. This also applies to **Glute Bridges** and **Step-ups!** Stay low and move slowly with control on your **Lateral Shuffle** – this will really work your glutes! In your **Fast Feet into High Knees,** jog on the spot for eight steps then increase your pace to a sprint and raise your knees to hip height. Return to a jog and repeat until time is up.

In your CORE exercises, draw your belly button to your spine at all times to keep your core engaged. Place your hands behind your head for your **Reaching Crunches** and **Lateral Scissors** if you feel your neck straining. In your **Lateral Scissors** move your legs in and out in a controlled, steady movement. Keep that controlled pace for your **Heel Taps** too.

SET 1 x 3 rounds

WIDE SQUATS
30 seconds (Slow, controlled)

SQUAT JUMPS
30 seconds (Fast, high intensity)

REVERSE LUNGES
20 seconds each side (Slow, controlled)

LATERAL SHUFFLE
45 seconds

1 minute rest after 3 repeats of SET 1

SET 2 — x 3 rounds

GLUTE BRIDGES
30 seconds (Slow, controlled)

FAST FEET INTO HIGH KNEES
30 seconds (Fast, high intensity)

STEP-UPS
60 seconds. Alternating sides. (Slow, controlled)

SKIP
60 seconds (Fast, high intensity)

CORE — x 3 rounds

REACHING CRUNCHES
30 seconds

3PT PLANK SET
20 seconds each position

Move your legs like scissors!

LATERAL SCISSORS
30 seconds

HEEL TAPS
30 seconds

Don't forget to warm up and warm down (see page 67).

1 minute rest after 3 repeats of SET 2

Week

1.

Upper Body

For your **Push-up Position Touches**, imagine your arms are the hands of a clock. Reach out to different points, keeping your core engaged and shoulders and hips level. Alternate sides in your **Up-down Plank** so you're working all your muscle groups. In the **Y to W**, activate between your shoulderblades by drawing your arms from a Y shape into a W shape. Keep your chest elevated and core engaged. Then, speed up for your **Mountain Climbers**!

In your **Bench Dips** your elbows want to be straight, not flared out. The **Surf Warrior Pop-up** is my version of a burpee! Keep a fast pace as you bounce between a high plank and your surf stance. Find a box or bench to challenge yourself in **Push-ups Hands Raised**. The higher the box, the easier it will be.

In a **Side Plank**, your shoulder should always be directly above your elbow. Aim to touch the tops of your knees when doing **Crunches**, and to touch elbow to opposite knee when doing **Bicycle Crunches**. The **Caterpillar** is an awesome core challenge! Walk your hands away from your feet as far as you can, then step your feet back in and repeat.

SET 1 x 3 rounds

Touch 12, 3 and 6 o'clock with your left hand, then 12, 9 and 6 o'clock with your right hand

PUSH-UP POSITION TOUCHES
40 seconds (Slow, controlled)

UP-DOWN PLANK
45 seconds (Fast, high intensity)

Y TO W
40 seconds (Slow, controlled)

MOUNTAIN CLIMBERS
45 seconds (Fast, high intensity)

1 minute rest after 3 repeats of SET 1

SET 2 x 3 rounds

BENCH DIPS – BENT LEGS
40 seconds (Slow, controlled)

SURF WARRIOR POP-UP
40 seconds (Fast, high intensity)

PUSH-UPS HANDS RAISED
40 seconds (Slow, controlled)

SKIP
60 seconds (Fast, high intensity)

CORE x 3 rounds

SIDE PLANKS
30 seconds each side

CRUNCHES
40 seconds

BICYCLE CRUNCHES
40 seconds

CATERPILLAR
45 seconds

Don't forget to warm up and warm down (see page 67).

1 minute rest after 3 repeats of SET 2

1.

Full Body

Your pyramid sets comprise of **Skipping** for 30 seconds then performing your resistance exercise for 30 seconds. Increase each rep by 10 seconds until you reach 50 seconds per exercise. Then work your way back down to 30 seconds per exercise. **Skipping** is one of my favourite exercises and I take my rope all around the world with me! If you don't have one, don't stress. You can skip on the spot, do fast feet, cross overs, high knees, toe taps, or any combination of high-energy movement that increases your heart rate.

Keep your core engaged when doing **Push-ups Hands Raised,** and remember to keep your elbows close to your body to challenge your triceps as well as your pecs.

The **Sumo Squat Hold** is a great way to open up your hips. Work on making your chest tall, with your feet pointed out slightly and knees tracking over your toes. And don't forget to breathe!

Around-the-world Crunches are an effective combo of heel tap, crunch, heel tap and reverse crunch. This works your entire core!

Grab a friend and alternate pyramid exercises, it's one of the best ways to stay motivated!

SET 1

Alternate between Skip and Push-ups Hands Raised

SKIP

PUSH-UP HANDS RAISED

30 seconds skipping then 30 seconds push-up
40 seconds skipping then 40 seconds push-up
50 seconds skipping then 50 seconds push-up
50 seconds skipping then 50 seconds push-up
40 seconds skipping then 40 seconds push-up
30 seconds skipping then 30 seconds push-up

1 minute rest after SET 1

SET 2

Alternate between Skip and Sumo Squat Hold

SKIP

SUMO SQUAT HOLD

30 seconds skipping then 30 seconds sumo squat
40 seconds skipping then 40 seconds sumo squat
50 seconds skipping then 50 seconds sumo squat
50 seconds skipping then 50 seconds sumo squat
40 seconds skipping then 40 seconds sumo squat
30 seconds skipping then 30 seconds sumo squat

SET 3

Alternate between Skip and Around-the-world Crunches

SKIP

AROUND-THE-WORLD CRUNCHES

30 seconds skipping then 30 seconds crunches
40 seconds skipping then 40 seconds crunches
50 seconds skipping then 50 seconds crunches
50 seconds skipping then 50 seconds crunches
40 seconds skipping then 40 seconds crunches
30 seconds skipping then 30 seconds crunches

I minute rest after SET 2

Don't forget to warm up and warm down (see page 67).

Week

2.

MINDFULNESS *is* EVERYTHING

This week, pay attention to how much you're eating, at what times and how it's making you feel. Record your meals, meal times and energy levels in a food diary and take note of any energy highs or lows. If you're running out of energy at the end of the day, you might need to add a protein-rich snack to your morning, such as a boiled egg or a smoothie with protein powder.

Sit down away from the TV or other screens to **focus on mindfully eating**, not rushing to finish your food. Our stomachs send messages to our brains to register that we are full, but eating too quickly can disrupt this pattern and result in us overeating, then suddenly feeling stuffed. If you catch yourself eating big mouthfuls, try swapping to chopsticks for a few meals and notice how a **slower pace** makes you feel.

It's not just what you eat, but when and how as well.

Shopping List

21 MEALS • SERVES 2

FRESH FAVOURITES

FRUIT, VEGETABLES AND HERBS

2 green apples
1 bunch asparagus
2 avocados
3 bananas
1 packet bean sprouts
1 punnet blueberries
1 head broccoli
¼ red cabbage
3 red capsicums
5 carrots
1 purple carrot
1 cauliflower
4 celery stalks
1 punnet cherry tomatoes
3 long red chillies
1 small red chilli
1 corn cob
5 Lebanese cucumbers
3 eggplants
12 cloves garlic
30 g ginger
1 jalapeno chilli
1 large bunch kale
2 kiwi fruit

4 cos lettuce leaves
4 lemons
4 limes
1 mango
1 cup (90 g) button mushrooms
4 field mushrooms
3 tablespoons (30 g) black olives
2 onions
2 red onions
½ pineapple
8 radishes
2 handfuls of rocket
2 handfuls of snowpeas
8 handfuls of baby spinach
1 bunch spring onions
1 punnet strawberries
½ cup (85 g) sultanas
1 sweet potato
2 x 400 g tins diced
   tomatoes
1 jar tomato paste
piece of fresh turmeric
1 wombok (Chinese) cabbage
3 large zucchini
1 bunch basil

1 bunch Thai basil
1 bay leaf
1 bunch coriander
1 bunch mint
1 bunch flat-leaf parsley
2 sprigs rosemary

MEAT, POULTRY AND SEAFOOD

500 g beef mince
400 g chicken breast
400 g chicken thigh fillets
200 g flathead tail
200 g ocean trout fillet
200 g pork fillet
200 g green (raw) prawns
200 g salmon fillet
2 x 95 g tins tuna in olive oil

EGGS AND DAIRY/ALTERNATIVES

10 organic eggs
1 cup (250 ml) coconut milk
350 g coconut yoghurt (or
   yoghurt of your choice)
250 g firm tofu
1 litre coconut water

PANTRY STAPLES

GRAINS, PULSES, NUTS AND SEEDS

3 tablespoons (35 g) buckwheat
   flour
1 packet rice paper rounds
150 g rice stick noodles
2 cups (190 g) rolled oats
2 cups (190 g) spelt flakes
1 packet wholegrain wraps
1 x 400 g tin chickpeas
½ cup (80 g) raw almonds
3 tablespoons (40 g) raw
   cashews
1 tablespoon (15 g) chia seeds

1½ cups (85 g) coconut flakes
¾ cup (115 g) pumpkin seeds
2 tablespoons (30 g) sesame
   seeds
½ cup (75 g) sunflower seeds
3 tablespoons (30 g) walnuts

SPICES, OILS AND CONDIMENTS

ground cardamom
ground ginger
rice wine vinegar
chai tea bags
pure vanilla extract

Week

2.

Monday

WEEK
2.

BREAKFAST

Broccoli and Pesto
Frittata

PAGE 141

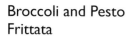

USE
LEFTOVERS
from SUN
BREAKFAST

LUNCH

Buckwheat, Strawberry
and Basil Salad

PAGE 201

*Your salad will
stay fresh if you
drizzle over the
dressing when
ready to serve!*

USE
LEFTOVERS
from SUN
LUNCH

DINNER

Satay Tofu Rice Paper Rolls

PAGE 254

Week

2.

Tuesday

BREAKFAST

LUNCH

DINNER

Kiwi, Avocado and Lime Smoothie Bowl with Homemade Muesli

PAGE 142

We'll use the leftover muesli later.

Zucchini Noodles with Rocket, Salmon and Hummus

PAGE 202

Chicken Pad Thai

PAGE 257

SAVE LEFTOVERS *for* WED LUNCH

Rise and shine

Getting up early is my favourite way to get a head start on the day. (Read more on page 16.) This week, try tweaking your schedule so that you can get more out of the day. Maybe you'll do your workout in your lunch break or meditate on your commute home. Write down one change you can try this week.

Wednesday

BREAKFAST

Chai Bircher Muesli

PAGE 145

Try making this one the night before!

LUNCH

Chicken Pad Thai

PAGE 257

USE LEFTOVERS *from* TUE DINNER

DINNER

Pork Fillet with Garlic Mushrooms and Apple Slaw

PAGE 258

Week

2.

Thursday

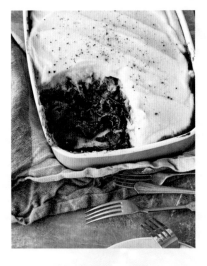

BREAKFAST

LUNCH

DINNER

Egg and Hummus on Sourdough with Cucumber, Celery, Pineapple and Mint Juice

PAGE 146

Tuna, Avo and Chilli Smash with Rainbow Veggies

PAGE 205

Beef and Eggplant Lasagne

PAGE 261

SAVE LEFTOVERS *for* **FRI LUNCH**

Make it count

This week's focus is timing so check in with yourself. Are you eating slowly and mindfully at meal times? Are you getting the most out of every day? Now's your chance to make any changes so list the areas you want to focus on.

....

....

....

....

Friday

BREAKFAST

Mango and Coconut Smoothie

PAGE 149

LUNCH

Beef and Eggplant Lasagne

PAGE 261

USE LEFTOVERS *from* THU DINNER

DINNER

Prawn and Broccoli Stir-Fry

PAGE 262

Week

2.

Saturday

BREAKFAST

Buckwheat Blueberry
Pancakes

PAGE 150

LUNCH

Creamy Chicken and
Spinach Wrap

PAGE 206

DINNER

Baked Ocean Trout with
Veggies and Kale Chips

PAGE 265

*I recommend making
extra kale chips
to nibble on!*

Wind it back

We all want to make the most of every day, but downtime is to well-being like workouts are to fitness. Make sure you take some time this weekend to recharge your batteries. Read up on my favourite ways to unwind on page 20 and write down your relaxation plans here.

Sunday

BREAKFAST

Greens with Eggs and Chilli

PAGE 153

LUNCH

Spicy Fish Tacos

PAGE 209

DINNER

Black Bean and Sweet Potato Nachos

PAGE 266

Week

2.

Lower Body

When doing **Scorpion Kicks** it's important to only extend your leg as high as you can without your pelvis tilting foward. If you experience any pain in your **Squat Jumps**, stick to normal squats. Keep your chest tall and knees tracking over your toes in your **Lunges**, never sacrifice form for speed. The **Athlete Skip** is a super explosive movement, drive your opposite arm and knee as high as you can, alternating sides.

In a **Squat Hold**, aim to keep your chest tall and concentrate on activating your glutes. How many **Burpees** can you do in 40 seconds? Keep count and try to beat it next week! In your **4pt Multi-directional Lunges**, imagine you are lunging forward to 12, 2, 4 and 6 o'clock. Then repeat on the other side to 6, 8, 10, 12 o'clock. This challenges different muscles – and your coordination!

Keep your core engaged and your neck long in your **Floor Cobra**. You should feel the muscles activating between your shoulderblades. The **Alternate Arm & Leg Reach** is a great way to activate your obliques. Aim to touch your toes then alternate sides.

SET 1 x 3 rounds

SCORPION KICKS
30 seconds each side (Slow, controlled)

SQUAT JUMPS
30 seconds (Fast, high intensity)

LUNGES
50 seconds alternating sides (Slow, controlled)

ATHLETE SKIP
40 seconds (Fast, high intensity)

1 minute rest after 3 repeats of SET 1

SET 2 x 3 rounds

CORE x 3 rounds

SQUAT HOLD
Hold for 30 seconds (Slow, controlled)

FLOOR COBRA
Hold for 30 seconds

BURPEES
30 seconds (Fast, high intensity)

MOUNTAIN CLIMBERS
30 seconds

4PT MULTI-DIRECTIONAL LUNGES
60 seconds (Slow, controlled)

Then repeat on other side!

ALTERNATE ARM & LEG REACH
40 seconds

SKIP
60 seconds (Fast, high intensity)

CRUNCHES TO HALFWAY
30 seconds

Don't forget to warm up and warm down (see page 67).

1 minute rest after 3 repeats of SET 2

Week

2.

Upper Body

We're kicking off with **Low Squat Aeroplane Arms** that works your whole body! Squat low, engage your core, and alternate tiny circles with your arms (forwards for 10, then back for 10). Focus on speed and extension in your **Star Jumps** – they'll get your heart rate firing! Next, you'll be holding a **Floor Cobra** position but drawing **Butterfly Scoops** – just like the shape of a butterfly wing – to really work your shoulders, just like we do in the **Y to W**. Engage your core, stay light on your toes and alternate your arms for **Punches in Front**.

Your **Bear Crawl** is about control, coordination and core engagement! Next, add a **Pulse** to your **Side Plank** and remember your alignment cues from page 70.

Aim to keep your knees directly above hips in **Crunches – Bent Legs** so that you're properly activating your core. You'll soon be a pro with **Lateral Scissors** and **Bicycle Crunches**! So lets add an extra challenge of **Flutter Kicks**. Lift your head and shoulders off the floor and keep your kicking movement small, drawing that belly button in the entire time.

LOW SQUAT AEROPLANE ARMS
45 seconds (Slow, controlled)

STAR JUMPS
45 seconds (Fast, high intensity)

BUTTERFLY SCOOPS
40 seconds (Slow, controlled)

PUNCHES IN FRONT
40 seconds (Fast, high intensity)

1 minute rest after 3 repeats of SET 1

SET 2 x 3 rounds

Y TO W
50 seconds (Slow, controlled)

BEAR CRAWL
45 seconds (Fast, high intensity)

SIDE PLANK PULSE
20 seconds each side

SKIP
60 seconds (Fast, high intensity)

I minute rest after 3 repeats of SET 2

CORE x 3 rounds

CRUNCHES – BENT LEGS
45 seconds

Move your legs like scissors!

LATERAL SCISSORS
45 seconds

BICYCLE CRUNCHES
40 seconds

Kick your feet up and down in short sharp strokes.

FLUTTER KICKS
45 seconds

Don't forget to warm up and warm down (see page 67).

2.

Full Body

As per Week 1, your pyramid sets comprise of **Skipping** for 30 seconds then performing your resistance exercise for 30 seconds. Increase each rep by 10 seconds until you reach 50 seconds per exercise. Then work your way back down to 30 seconds per exercise.

As you **Bench Dip – Bent Legs**, keep your focus on bringing your butt close to the bench – it will make it harder and more effective! You can also extend your legs out straight if you're ready for an extra challenge.

In your **4pt Multi-directional Lunges**, focus on control and landing softly with each step. You should feel this in your glutes, quads and hamstrings!

The last set is all about core with your **Crunches – Bent Legs**. Aim to initiate the movement from your core and avoid straining through your neck and shoulders. Exhale as you crunch up and inhale as you lower down.

Twenty-four minutes of work – let's smash it!

SET 1

Alternate Skip and Bench Dips – Bent Legs

SKIP

BENCH DIPS – BENT LEGS

30 seconds skipping then 30 seconds bench dips
40 seconds skipping then 40 seconds bench dips
50 seconds skipping then 50 seconds bench dips
50 seconds skipping then 50 seconds bench dips
40 seconds skipping then 40 seconds bench dips
30 seconds skipping then 30 seconds bench dips

1 minute rest after SET 1

SET 2

Alternate Skip and 4pt Multi-directional Lunges

SKIP

Make sure you lunge on both sides every round!

4PT MULTI-DIRECTIONAL LUNGES

30 seconds skipping then 30 seconds lunges
40 seconds skipping then 40 seconds lunges
50 seconds skipping then 50 seconds lunges
50 seconds skipping then 50 seconds lunges
40 seconds skipping then 40 seconds lunges
30 seconds skipping then 30 seconds lunges

1 minute rest after SET 2

SET 3

Alternate Skip and Crunches – Bent Legs

SKIP

CRUNCHES – BENT LEGS

30 seconds skipping then 30 seconds crunches
40 seconds skipping then 40 seconds crunches
50 seconds skipping then 50 seconds crunches
50 seconds skipping then 50 seconds crunches
40 seconds skipping then 40 seconds crunches
30 seconds skipping then 30 seconds crunches

Don't forget to warm up and warm down (see page 67).

Week

3.

RECHARGE *your* BATTERIES

Where are you expending most of your energy? Are you giving time and effort to the things that **really matter** to you, or are you worrying about things that are outside your control? This week, take a moment to think about where your energy goes. If you need to make an adjustment, start with small increments and then build from there.

You are not a machine! You don't have an endless supply of energy. It's important to stop and **recharge regularly**. In this fast-paced world, taking time out for rest and quiet contemplation seems impossible sometimes – but the value of some **daily downtime** cannot be overestimated.

Rest, recharge and do something for yourself each and every day.

Shopping List

21 MEALS • SERVES 2

FRESH FAVOURITES

FRUIT, VEGETABLES AND HERBS
2 red apples
2 bunches asparagus
2 avocados
3 bananas
1 packet bean sprouts
2 beetroots
2 cups (about 400 g) mixed
   berries
1 head broccoli
1 red capsicum
3 carrots
1 cauliflower
4 Lebanese cucumbers
½ cup (75 g) currants
4 celery stalks
6 chat potatoes
2 punnets cherry tomatoes
1 long green chilli
2 long red chillies
2 medjool dates
2 fresh figs
6 cloves garlic
10 g ginger
2 handfuls of green grapes
3 handfuls of green beans
1 small bunch kale
1 kent (jap) pumpkin

2 kiwi fruit
5 lemons
6 cos lettuce leaves
5 handfuls of mixed lettuce
1 lime
2 cups (180 g) button
   mushrooms
3 tablespoons (30 g) black olives
2 onions
1 red onion
3 oranges
2 passionfruit
1½ cups (230 g) peas
¼ pineapple
1 pomegranate
2 handfuls of rocket
1 bunch silverbeet
2 handfuls of snowpeas
9 handfuls of baby spinach
1 bunch spring onions
2 handfuls of sugar snap peas
2 sweet potatoes
1 zucchini
1 bunch basil
1 bunch coriander
1 handful of fresh curry leaves
1 bunch mint
1 bunch flat-leaf parsley

2 sprigs rosemary
6 sprigs thyme

MEAT, POULTRY AND SEAFOOD
800 g chicken breast
400 g chicken thigh fillets
200 g eye fillet
200 g lamb cutlets
250 g lamb mince
250 g turkey mince
200 g barramundi fillet
2 x 125 g tins mackerel fillets
200 g salmon fillet
200 g smoked salmon
200 g firm white fish fillet

EGGS AND DAIRY/ALTERNATIVES
15 organic eggs
200 g haloumi
1 x 400 g tin organic, full-fat
   coconut milk
1¾ cups (440 ml) milk of your
   choice
195 g coconut yoghurt (or
   yoghurt of your choice)

PANTRY STAPLES

GRAINS, PULSES, NUTS AND SEEDS
½ cup (110 g) buckwheat groats
1½ cups (285 g) wholegrain
   couscous
½ cup (100 g) white quinoa
¾ cup (140 g) brown rice
1 x 400 g tin chickpeas
¾ cup (120 g) raw almonds
½ cup (80 g) chia seeds

2 cups (110 g) coconut flakes
3 tablespoons (40 g) dukkah
3 tablespoons (40 g)
   sesame seeds
⅓ cup (40 g) walnuts

SPICES, OILS AND CONDIMENTS
fennel seeds
brown mustard seeds

*Just another reminder
to check your pantry
before shopping for these
ingredients!*

3.

Monday

BREAKFAST

LUNCH

DINNER

Pumpkin and Rosemary
Frittatas with Cucumber,
Celery and Mint Juice

PAGES 154 & 146

SAVE
LEFTOVERS
for WED
LUNCH

Quinoa, Sweet Potato and
Apple Salad

PAGE 209

Barramundi with Roast
Pumpkin, Asparagus and
Pomegranate

PAGE 269

*Make a head start on
Tuesday's breakfast
by soaking your
porridge overnight.*

Week

3.

Tuesday

BREAKFAST

Apple and Date Buckwheat
Porridge with Figs

PAGE 157

LUNCH

Fried Brown Rice with Fish

PAGE 213

DINNER

Lamb Koftas with
Cauliflower Pilaf

PAGE 270

Catch those zzzs

Sleep is one of the best ways to recharge our bodies and minds. (Read more on page 45.) Are you getting enough? Record how many hours shut-eye you're getting this week and track your energy levels.

MONDAY: ....

TUESDAY: ....

WEDNESDAY: ....

THURSDAY: ....

FRIDAY: ....

SATURDAY: ....

SUNDAY: ....

Wednesday

BREAKFAST

Kiwi and Greens Smoothie

PAGE 158

LUNCH

Pumpkin and Rosemary Frittatas

PAGE 154

Serve with 1 handful mixed lettuce and 1 cup cherry tomatoes.

USE LEFTOVERS *from* MON BREAKFAST

DINNER

Chicken and Grape Salad

PAGE 273

SAVE LEFTOVERS *for* THU LUNCH

3.

Thursday

USE
LEFTOVERS
from WED
DINNER

BREAKFAST

Spinach and Mushroom
Fry-Up with Boiled Eggs

PAGE 161

LUNCH

Chicken and Grape Salad

PAGE 273

DINNER

Baked Lemon Fish with
Sweet Potato Mash and
Mixed Peas

PAGE 274

Powerful pals

Think about the people in your life who inspire you and spread positive energy. My best friend, Christine, and I don't see each other very often but she's always there for me and when we send meaningful photos to each other, it always puts a smile on my face. This weekend, make it your mission to connect with the positive people in your life.

Friday

BREAKFAST

Berry and Passionfruit Smoothie Bowl

PAGE 162

Mix in some protein powder if you've just done a workout!

LUNCH

Smoked Salmon and Sesame Salad

PAGE 214

DINNER

Dukkah-Crusted Steak with Beet Chips and Green Beans

PAGE 277

3.

Saturday

BREAKFAST

Banana, Almond Butter
and Berry Jam on Toast

PAGE 165

LUNCH

Chicken, Chickpea and
Roast Tomato Salad

PAGE 217

DINNER

Turkey Meatball Green
Curry

PAGE 278

Rest and reflect

How did you go tracking your sleep this week? Did you get enough zzzs? The end of the week is the perfect time to reflect on positive habits and commit to those you want to maintain. Make yourself a cup of tea, find a quiet corner and take a moment to write down your plan for looking after your energy levels.

Sunday

BREAKFAST

Green Pesto Omelette

PAGE 166

LUNCH

Lamb Cutlets with Turmeric Couscous and Silverbeet

PAGE 218

DINNER

Salmon Nicoise Platter

PAGE 281

Week 3.

Lower Body

Try a new squat this week with **Narrow Squats**. Bring your feet just inside hip-width apart, and ensure your knees are tracking straight as you lower. See how high you can go with fast and light **High Knees**! Keep your core engaged and hips level with **Donkey Kicks**. Activate your glutes as you raise one leg with the knee bent at 90 degrees. For the **Bunny Hops**, press through the ground, engage your core and aim to get some hang time at the top of the movement.

Get your training buddy or a mirror to check your **Glute Bridges**. You want to lift your hips to make a straight line from your knees to shoulders. Fire up your legs by staying upright as you pop up into your **Surf Warrior**. At the top of your **Step-ups**, drive opposite elbow and knee in a running motion to take it to the next level.

Choose a variation of the **Hold in Dish** that's right for you and don't forget to breathe! Once you've nailed the **Bicycle Crunches** up the ante and focus on speed. As your core strengthens, focus on keeping your shoulders, hips and knees in a straight line for your **Mountain Climbers** and **High Plank Hold**.

SET 1 x 3 rounds

NARROW SQUATS
30 seconds (Slow, controlled)

HIGH KNEES
30 seconds (Fast, high intensity)

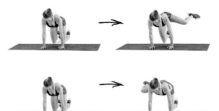

DONKEY KICKS
30 seconds each side

BUNNY HOPS
40 seconds (Fast, high intensity)

1 minute rest after 3 repeats of SET 1

Option 2 is harder!

or

HOLD IN DISH
Hold for 20 seconds

GLUTE BRIDGES
Hold for 40 seconds (Slow, controlled)

SURF WARRIOR POP-UPS
45 seconds (Fast, high intensity)

BICYCLE CRUNCHES
30 seconds (Fast, high intensity)

STEP-UPS
40 seconds, alternating sides (Alternate legs; slow, controlled)

MOUNTAIN CLIMBERS
30 seconds (Slow, controlled)

SKIP
60 seconds (Fast, high intensity)

HIGH PLANK HOLD
Hold for 30 seconds

Don't forget to warm up and warm down (see page 67).

I minute rest after 3 repeats of SET 2

Week

3.

Upper Body

Lower your elbows to a 90-degree angle with every rep of your Bench Dips. Once you've nailed your **Bear Crawl**, try the same movement but faster for an extra challenge!

Imagine you are pushing your hands through the ground and keep your shoulders stacked directly over wrists when in a **High Plank Hold** to avoid collapsing your shoulders. If you want to mix up your **Mountain Climbers**, try touching knee to opposite elbow to challenge your obliques.

Up the ante on your **Push-ups** this week by removing the box. Exhale as you lower, engaging your core to support you. Do you remember your **Burpee** count from last week? And how does your **Caterpillar** compare to Week 1?

Just like in a regular plank, your body for your **Side Plank** should be in a straight line through hips and knees, all the way to your toes. When doing **Heel Taps** keep your knees directly over hips and the movement slow and controlled. This and your **Reverse Crunch with Leg Lower** will really challenge your lower abs. We're also increasing the **Crunches** challenge by moving up to **Straight Legs**!

SET 1 x 3 rounds

BENCH DIPS – STRAIGHT LEGS
40 seconds (Slow, controlled)

Forwards and backwards!

BEAR CRAWL
40 seconds (Fast, high intensity)

HIGH PLANK HOLD
Hold for 40 seconds (Slow, controlled)

MOUNTAIN CLIMBERS
40 seconds (Fast, high intensity)

I minute rest after 3 repeats of SET 1

PUSH-UPS
40 seconds (Slow, controlled)

SIDE PLANK
35 seconds each side

BURPEES
40 seconds (Fast, high intensity)

HEEL TAPS
40 seconds

CATERPILLAR
40 seconds (Slow, controlled)

CRUNCHES – STRAIGHT LEGS
40 seconds

SKIP
60 seconds (Fast, high intensity)

REVERSE CRUNCH WITH LEG LOWER
40 seconds

Don't forget to warm up and warm down (see page 67).

I minute rest after 3 repeats of SET 2

Week
3.

Full Body

Your Week 3 pyramid set is a little different to previous weeks. It comprises of **Skipping** for 15 seconds then performing your resistance exercise for 15 seconds. Increase each rep by 15 seconds until you reach 60 seconds per exercise. Then work your way back down to 15 seconds per exercise.

Now that you're past halfway in the plan, try adding in some different **Skipping** styles. I love mixing it up from regular skips to high-knee skips, double unders and cross overs. Through your **Up-down Plank**, focus on maintaining the momentum. Move with your breath; lowering on the inhale and pushing up on the exhale.

You've got a new exercise this week: **Frog Squats!** Start with your feet wide, toes pointed slightly outwards in a low squat with your hands clasped in front. Without letting your knees roll in, raise your butt to straighten your legs, then come back down. Keep it slow and controlled – you should feel this in your hamstrings, quads and glutes!

Keep reaching high in every single rep of your **Alternate Arm & Leg Reach**, making sure the other arm and leg stay on the ground.

Don't stop when it hurts . . . stop when you're done!

SET 1

Alternate Skip and Up-down Plank

Skip

UP-DOWN PLANK

15 seconds skipping then 15 seconds plank
30 seconds skipping then 30 seconds plank
45 seconds skipping then 45 seconds plank
60 seconds skipping then 60 seconds plank
45 seconds skipping then 45 seconds plank
30 seconds skipping then 30 seconds plank
15 seconds skipping then 15 seconds plank

1 minute rest after SET 1

SET 2

Alternate Skip and Frog Squats

Skip

FROG SQUAT

15 seconds skipping then 15 seconds frog squat
30 seconds skipping then 30 seconds frog squat
45 seconds skipping then 45 seconds frog squat
60 seconds skipping then 60 seconds frog squat
45 seconds skipping then 45 seconds frog squat
30 seconds skipping then 30 seconds frog squat
15 seconds skipping then 15 seconds frog squat

SET 3

Alternate Skip and Alternate Arm & Leg Reach

Skip

ALTERNATE ARM & LEG REACH

15 seconds skipping then 15 seconds arm & leg reach
30 seconds skipping then 30 seconds arm & leg reach
45 seconds skipping then 45 seconds arm & leg reach
60 seconds skipping then 60 seconds arm & leg reach
45 seconds skipping then 45 seconds arm & leg reach
30 seconds skipping then 30 seconds arm & leg reach
15 seconds skipping then 15 seconds arm & leg reach

I minute rest after SET 2

Don't forget to warm up and warm down (see page 67).

Week

4.

Expand your horizons in your body AND your mind.

DISCOVER *new ways* TO MOVE

We are all designed to move! Spending hours sitting at a desk is detrimental to our posture, health, wellness and happiness. Whether you are exercising regularly, or not at all, this week look for a **new take on movement**. If you're a regular in the gym pumping weights, try getting outside for a cruisy walk in the park. Or if you love running, try something that challenges your balance and coordination like surfing or boxing.

If you operate at high speed all day, every day, try **unwinding** with some yoga. Challenging our bodies isn't always about **harder, faster, stronger**. Broadening our horizons to find new ways to move can unlock new experiences and skills that we didn't know were possible!

Shopping List

21 MEALS • SERVES 2

FRESH FAVOURITES

FRUIT, VEGETABLES AND HERBS

2 green apples
1 bunch asparagus
2 avocados
1 banana
1 beetroot
½ cup (100 g) mixed berries
½ cup (80 g) blueberries
1 green capsicum
1 red capsicum
5 carrots
1 bunch baby heirloom carrots
1 cauliflower
2 punnets cherry tomatoes
1 punnet vine-ripened cherry
    tomatoes
1 tomato
1 small jar tomato paste
1 long green chilli
2 long red chillies
1 small red chilli
1 corn cob
2 Lebanese cucumbers
½ cup (75 g) currants

7 cloves garlic
1 grapefruit
1 handful of green grapes
1 bunch kale
1 kiwi fruit
1 iceberg lettuce
1 handful of mixed lettuce
3 lemons
2 limes
1 packet mung beans
1 onion
2 red onions
1 orange
4 passionfruit
1 peach
2 pears
1 pomegranate
1 radicchio
1 bunch radishes
8 handfuls of rocket
4 handfuls of baby spinach
2 sweet potatoes
piece of fresh turmeric
½ wombok (Chinese) cabbage

1 bunch coriander
1 bunch mint
1 bunch flat-leaf parsley

MEAT, POULTRY AND SEAFOOD

250 g beef mince
800 g chicken breast
800 g chicken thigh fillets
250 g lamb mince
200 g pork cutlets
2 x 125 g tins mackerel fillets
500 g mussels
100 g smoked salmon
200 g tuna fillet (or 2 x 95 g tins)
200 g white fish fillet

EGGS AND DAIRY/ALTERNATIVES

13 organic eggs
1 litre coconut milk
1 x 400 g tin organic, full-fat
    coconut milk
350 g coconut yoghurt (or
    yoghurt of your choice)

PANTRY STAPLES

GRAINS, PULSES, NUTS AND SEEDS

2 wholegrain bread rolls
250 g wholegrain spaghetti
¾ cup (140 g) brown rice
2 x 400 g tins chickpeas
1 x 400 g tin brown lentils
1⅓ cups (200 g) raw cashews
½ cup (45 g) desiccated
    coconut
½ cup (80 g) dukkah
¾ cup (100 g) raw pistachio
    kernels
3 tablespoons (30 g) walnuts

SPICES, OILS AND CONDIMENTS

raw cacao powder
harissa spice blend
protein powder

Plus 2 x wholegrain wraps frozen in Week 2 – we'll be using them on Saturday!

Week

4.

Monday

BREAKFAST

Pear and Blueberry
Smoothie

PAGE 169

LUNCH

Mackerel and Cauliflower
Couscous Salad

PAGE 221

DINNER

Falafels with Green Sauce
in Lettuce Cups

PAGE 282

SAVE
LEFTOVERS
for TUE
LUNCH

4.

Tuesday

BREAKFAST

Coconut Yoghurt with
Muesli and Passionfruit

PAGE 170

LUNCH

Falafels with Green Sauce
in Lettuce Cups

PAGE 282

USE
LEFTOVERS
from MON
DINNER

DINNER

Harissa Fish with Radish
and Roast Carrot Salad

PAGE 285

Plan of attack

The first step to achieving your goals is planning them! Just like you did with your daily rituals in Week 1, plan the workouts you're going to tackle this week. Aim to move for at least half an hour every day, and complete your #fitz workouts every other day to allow your body to rest and recover.

MONDAY: ....

TUESDAY: ....

WEDNESDAY: ....

THURSDAY: ....

FRIDAY: ....

SATURDAY: ....

SUNDAY: ....

Wednesday

BREAKFAST

Coconut Scrambled Eggs with Asparagus on Toast

PAGE 173

LUNCH

Carrot and Coconut Slaw with Shredded Chicken

PAGE 222

DINNER

Open Lamb Burgers with Coconut Sauce

PAGE 286

Week

4.

Thursday

BREAKFAST

LUNCH

DINNER

Green Fruit Salad with
Cashew Cream

PAGE 174

*We'll use some
leftover Cashew
Cream on Sunday.*

Creamy Egg Cabbage Rolls

PAGE 225

Chicken Skewers with
Carrot, Beet and Apple
Salad

PAGE 289

SAVE
LEFTOVERS
for FRI
LUNCH

Stretch sesh

Every night, I have a stretching routine which helps me evaluate my body. (Read more on page 21.) It's a chance to re-align and stay on top of any niggles before they turn into injuries. Write down any areas that are feeling sore or tight, and take 10 minutes each night to give back to your body.

PROBLEM AREA:

THOUGHTS:

Friday

BREAKFAST

Pre-Workout Smoothie

PAGE 177

Head to pages 116-121 for this week's workouts!

LUNCH

Chicken Skewers with Carrot, Beet and Apple Salad

PAGE 289

USE LEFTOVERS *from* THU DINNER

DINNER

Mussel Spaghetti with Tomatoes and Garlic

PAGE 290

4.

Saturday

BREAKFAST

Smoked Salmon Egg Muffins
with Roast Tomatoes

PAGE 178

LUNCH

Tuna and Mung Bean Salad

PAGE 226

DINNER

Mustard Pork with Roast
Pear Salad

PAGE 293

Nature play

I'm a firm believer that fitness is about nourishing your mind as well as your body! This weekend, get out of the gym, step away from the stopwatch, and find a fun activity in nature: hiking, surfing, swimming, paddleboarding, walking your dog, anything! Soak up the vitamin D and enjoy your freedom under the sun.

Sunday

BREAKFAST

Avocado on Toast with Cashew Cream and Passionfruit

PAGE 181   *Uses leftover Cashew Cream from Thursday*

LUNCH

Citrus Salad with Lentils and Rocket

PAGE 229

DINNER

Mexican Beef with Salsa

PAGE 294

Week 4.

Lower Body

It's the final week of workouts! How are you going to challenge yourself? Why not try a slightly higher box for your **Step-ups** and **Box Jumps**? Keep your chest tall and lunge long in your **Reverse Lunges** – let your back knee kiss the floor with each rep to really make it count. Stay light and quick on your toes for the **Boxer Shuffle**, this one is all about speed.

To really nail your **Crab Walks**, lower into a narrow squat with your core engaged and chest tall. Take a small step to one side and transfer your weight without lifting out of your squat. Crab walk in one direction for half the time, then come back the other way. Pick up the pace again for **Cross Overs**, jumping out and then in, crossing a different leg in front each time. If you're ready to make your **Glute Bridge** harder, lift one leg off the ground for 20 seconds then switch legs at halfway.

The **Slow Negative Sit-ups** are all about control, lowering at the same pace and not collapsing on the floor. Exhale as you lower. Sit back up quickly, and repeat. We're working upper and lower abs as well as your back for the rest of your CORE set. Focus on your rhythm and making the most of it – it's under 8 minutes!

SET I x 3 rounds

STEP-UPS
50 seconds, alternating sides (Slow, controlled)

BOX JUMPS
30 seconds (Fast, high intensity)

REVERSE LUNGES
30 seconds each side (Slow, controlled)

BOXER SHUFFLE
30 seconds (Fast, high intensity)

I minute rest after 3 repeats of SET I

SLOW NEGATIVE SIT-UPS
35 seconds

CRAB WALKS
20 seconds each direction (Slow, controlled)

CRUNCHES TO HALFWAY
35 seconds

CROSS OVERS
35 seconds (Fast, high intensity)

FLOOR COBRA
Hold for 35 seconds (Slow, controlled)

GLUTE BRIDGE
Hold for 40 seconds (Slow, controlled)

HEEL TAPS
40 seconds

SKIP
60 seconds (Fast, high intensity)

Don't forget to warm up and warm down (see page 67).

1 minute rest after 3 repeats of SET 2

Week

4.

Upper Body

For the **Bent Over Fly**, keep your core engaged and raise your arms quickly, leading with the elbow. Then lower slowly, feeling the muscles in your back and shoulders activate. Aim for extension and speed in your **Star Jumps** – keep that momentum up! The **Y to W** works your upper back, but also engages your glutes and core for control and stability. Now that you're familiar with the **Bear Crawl**, see if you can pick up the pace!

Focus on keeping your weight in your heels in your **Low Squat Aeroplane Arms** and keep those arm circles small and fast! We're going for high **Punches in Front Above Head** this week. Bend your knees and engage your core for a stable foundation in which you can fire up your upper body. Press firmly through your supporting arm in your **Push-up Position Touches**, this will help you keep your hips even.

Get ready to work your obliques in this CORE set! All of these exercise will challenge your stabilising muscles which not only builds a leaner mid-section, but improves your form in other movements.

Remember - if it doesn't challenge you, it won't change you!

SET 1 x 3 rounds

BENT OVER FLY
45 seconds (Slow, controlled)

STAR JUMPS
45 seconds (Fast, high intensity)

Y TO W
25 seconds each side (Slow, controlled)

Forwards and backwards!

BEAR CRAWL
65 seconds (Fast, high intensity)

I minute rest after 3 repeats of SET 1

LOW SQUAT AEROPLANE ARMS
40 seconds (Slow, controlled)

HEEL TAPS
20 seconds each position

PUNCHES IN FRONT ABOVE HEAD
40 seconds (Fast, high intensity)

AROUND-THE-WORLD CRUNCHES
45 seconds

PUSH-UP POSITION TOUCHES
45 seconds (Alternate arms; slow, controlled)

SIDE PLANK
35 seconds each side (Slow, controlled)

SKIP
60 seconds (Fast, high intensity)

BICYCLE CRUNCHES
40 seconds

Don't forget to warm up and warm down (see page 67).

I minute rest after 3 repeats of SET 2

Week 4.

Full Body

Your final pyramid sets comprise of **Skipping** for 15 seconds then performing your resistance exercise for 15 seconds. Increase each rep by 15 seconds until you reach 60 seconds per exercise. Then work your way back down to 15 seconds per exercise.

Your final Full-body workout combines some of my favourite functional (and fun!) exercises in one workout. I hope that by now you're feeling confident in your technique with these movements and can focus on speed and control as you feel yourself getting stronger.

For more workouts like these, come and join me on the All Australian Beach Body app! I love sharing my training with you guys and hearing all about your workouts and progress. Stay in touch with me by following @allaustralianbeachbody on Instagram and Facebook, and using the hashtag #trainlikesally.

SET 1

Alternate Skip and Surf Warrior Pop-up

SKIP

SURF WARRIOR POP-UP

15 seconds skipping then 15 seconds pop-ups
30 seconds skipping then 30 seconds pop-ups
45 seconds skipping then 45 seconds pop-ups
60 seconds skipping then 60 seconds pop-ups
45 seconds skipping then 45 seconds pop-ups
30 seconds skipping then 30 seconds pop-ups
15 seconds skipping then 15 seconds pop-ups

1 minute rest after SET 1

WIN!

Share your FITZ workouts with me using #summerfit – I'll be drawing one
winner every month who'll score a lifetime membership to my AABB app!
Follow me @allaustralianbeachbody to see if you're a winner!

Terms and conditions at allaustralianbeachbody.com

SET 2

Alternate Skip and Crab Walk

SKIP

Switch direction halfway through duration

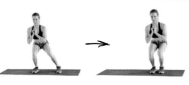

CRAB WALK

15 seconds skipping then 15 seconds crab walk
30 seconds skipping then 30 seconds crab walk
45 seconds skipping then 45 seconds crab walk
60 seconds skipping then 60 seconds crab walk
45 seconds skipping then 45 seconds crab walk
30 seconds skipping then 30 seconds crab walk
15 seconds skipping then 15 seconds crab walk

1 minute rest after SET 2

SET 3

Alternate Skip and Slow Negative Sit-ups

SKIP

SLOW NEGATIVE SIT-UPS

15 seconds skipping then 15 seconds sit-ups
30 seconds skipping then 30 seconds sit-ups
45 seconds skipping then 45 seconds sit-ups
60 seconds skipping then 60 seconds sit-ups
45 seconds skipping then 45 seconds sit-ups
30 seconds skipping then 30 seconds sit-ups
15 seconds skipping then 15 seconds sit-ups

Don't forget to warm up and warm down (see page 67).

MY
Recipes

LET'S EAT!

THERE ARE A FEW THINGS TO KNOW before you start cooking. To make your time in the kitchen as simple as possible, the recipes follow the same structure as the 4-week plan: Breakfast, Lunch and Dinner from Week 1 Monday to Week 4 Sunday. If you are following the 4-week plan, the coloured tabs will help you find the recipe you're looking for:

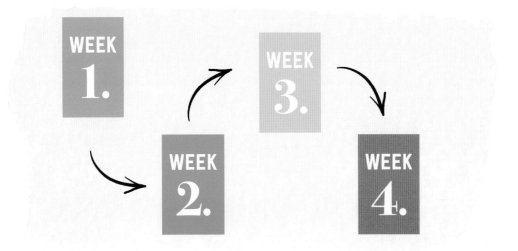

Keep an eye out for this leftovers symbol. It highlights recipes that serve four rather than two. It's such a handy feature as it gives you the heads-up to set half aside to eat later. No prep required!

The best thing about these recipes is that all of them can be enjoyed even if you aren't doing the 4-week plan and just want to eat healthier food. In each section, you'll see that after the meal plan recipes, there are some bonus meals that are close to my heart. And, of course, don't forget the Snacks and Desserts section, which is filled with yummy snacks and healthy treats!

I hope that my recipes will help you stay inspired in the kitchen and keep your tastebuds satisfied!

SHARE YOUR PICS AND WIN!

Share your amazing creations on Instagram using #summerfit to go in the draw to win a lifetime membership to my AABB app! Follow me @allaustralianbeachbody to see if you've been drawn.

Terms and conditions at allaustralianbeachbody.com

Breakfast

Figs are one of my all-time favourite fruits! If they're not in season, you can swap for 3 tablespoons of your favourite berries.

BANANA *and* FIG SALTED CARAMEL SMOOTHIE

SERVES 2

Start the week right with this deliciously creamy combo. Bananas are a great source of potassium, magnesium, fibre and amino acids, which can help to elevate our mood and therefore our happiness. Tahini, a paste made from ground sesame seeds, is rich in calcium. You can choose from hulled or unhulled tahini – I prefer hulled as it's creamier and less bitter. Add more almond milk or water to reach your preferred smoothie consistency. Top tip: peel and halve your bananas and freeze them in a container between sheets of baking paper to make your prep super-easy.

1 frozen banana
1 fresh fig
2 tablespoons tahini
2 teaspoons honey
2 teaspoons freshly squeezed
  lemon juice
pinch of sea salt
3 cups almond milk (or milk
  of your choice)

Place all the ingredients in a high-speed blender and blend until smooth.

ORANGE *and* ALMOND CHIA PUDDING

SERVES 2

Make this recipe the night before for a super-fast start to your day. You may like to test the consistency before you eat this – chia seeds absorb a lot of liquid so you might need to add a splash more almond milk or orange juice. If making this in the morning, allow a few hours for the chia seeds to absorb the milk and juice, and turn into a deliciously thick pudding.

1¼ cups almond milk
   (or milk of your choice)
½ cup freshly squeezed
   orange juice
finely grated zest and segments
   of 1 orange
2 tablespoons maple syrup
½ cup chia seeds
2 tablespoons raw almonds
½ green apple, finely sliced

Whisk the almond milk, orange juice and zest, maple syrup and chia seeds in a bowl. Wait for 5 minutes and whisk again, then again in another 5 minutes.

Pour into individual cups and set in the fridge for at least 2 hours (overnight is best), stirring during this time if needed to break up the chia seeds.

Top with the orange segments, almonds and apple to serve.

You can mix and match fresh fruit toppings and your favourite nuts.

Start your day with a party on your plate, thanks to this fresh, juicy and colourful salsa!

SMOKED SALMON *and* CORN SALSA *on* SOURDOUGH

SERVES 2

Avocados are nutritional powerhouses, containing a range of different vitamins and minerals as well as providing us with a hit of healthy fats and fibre. While I love filling out my meals with veg, I believe there is always room for good-quality bread in a balanced diet! Slice the leftover sourdough loaf up and keep it in the freezer.

1 corn cob, husk removed
½ cup cherry tomatoes, halved
   or quartered
½ avocado, diced
2 tablespoons chopped
   coriander, plus extra to serve
finely grated zest and juice
   of 1 lime
1 tablespoon extra virgin
   olive oil
sea salt and freshly ground
   black pepper
2 slices of sourdough toast
200 g smoked salmon

Set a steamer over a saucepan of gently boiling water. Place the corn in the steamer and steam for 2–3 minutes until just tender. Rinse the corn under cold water, then cut off the kernels.

Combine the tomatoes, avocado, corn and coriander in a bowl and gently stir through the lime zest and juice, olive oil and a good pinch of salt and pepper.

Serve the corn salsa on top of the toast with the smoked salmon and extra coriander.

BANGIN' BERRY SMOOTHIE

SERVES 2

When I have to be on the road in the morning, I love preparing and freezing my smoothies the night before. The berries in this recipe give us a big dose of antioxidants, while the almond butter incorporates essential healthy fats. We're also ticking off slow-releasing carbs with the oats, especially when combined with fibre-rich psyllium husk.

1 cup fresh or frozen mixed
   blueberries and blackberries,
   plus extra to serve (optional)
½ cup rolled oats, plus extra
   to serve (optional)
2 tablespoons almond butter
2 tablespoons psyllium husk
2 teaspoons honey
2 cups almond milk (or milk
   of your choice)
flaked coconut, to serve
   (optional)

Combine all the ingredients and 1 cup of water in a high-speed blender and blend until you reach your desired consistency. Top with extra berries, oats and/or flaked coconut.

Make your own almond butter

Simply whiz whole blanched almonds in a high-speed blender until the nuts release their oils and form a butter. You can add a touch of olive oil if needed, but the natural oils should be enough.

GRILLED PINEAPPLE *with* COCONUT YOGHURT *and* MINT

SERVES 2

You can fall even more in love with deliciously sweet pineapple knowing its vitamin-C levels can help boost your immunity, plus it contains an enzyme that aids in reducing inflammation. If pineapple isn't in season, swap it for kiwi fruit, which is also packed with vitamin C. Feel free to replace the coconut yoghurt for your regular favourite yoghurt, but always check the label for additives, preservatives and added sugar.

¼ pineapple, cut into four slices

2 tablespoons finely chopped mint, plus extra to serve

1 teaspoon coconut sugar

1 tablespoon desiccated coconut

1 teaspoon freshly squeezed lime juice

4 heaped tablespoons coconut yoghurt (or yoghurt of your choice)

3 tablespoons raw almonds, roughly chopped

Heat a char-grill pan over high heat and char-grill the pineapple for about 2 minutes on each side or until grill marks appear. Meanwhile, combine the mint, sugar, coconut and lime juice in a small dish and mix well, crushing the mint into the sugar.

Serve the grilled pineapple topped with coconut yoghurt and scatter over the almonds, and the mint and coconut mixture, and extra mint to serve.

PUMPKIN *and* CRANBERRY LOAF

MAKES 10 SLICES

Weekend bake-ups are so good for the soul! This is such a handy recipe as the loaf will keep for a week in the fridge, or you can slice and freeze it for up to a month, just taking out a slice and toasting it when needed: leftovers are perfect for snacks. (If keeping the loaf in the freezer, place some baking paper between each slice.) The seed topping and tahini boosts the protein content to make this a complete meal.

½ butternut pumpkin
  (about 280 g), peeled and
  diced into 2 cm cubes
3 tablespoons freshly squeezed
  orange juice
1 cup almond meal
1 cup rolled oats
½ cup buckwheat flour
1 tablespoon psyllium husk
¼ teaspoon sea salt
1 teaspoon baking powder
¼ teaspoon bicarbonate of soda
1 teaspoon ground cinnamon
¼ teaspoon ground nutmeg
2 organic eggs
3 tablespoons coconut oil,
  melted
3 tablespoons maple syrup
3 tablespoons walnuts,
  coarsely chopped
½ cup dried cranberries
1 tablespoon pumpkin seeds
1 tablespoon chia seeds
½ cup strawberries,
  hulled and sliced
tahini and/or honey, to serve
  (optional)

Preheat the oven to 180°C.

Grease a loaf tin and line it with baking paper.

Place the pumpkin in a steamer set over a saucepan of gently boiling water, and steam until very soft, about 12–15 minutes. Transfer to a food processor or high-speed blender, then add the orange juice and blend until smooth. Set aside to cool for 5 minutes.

Combine the almond meal, oats, buckwheat flour, psyllium husk, salt, baking powder, bicarbonate of soda, cinnamon and nutmeg in a large bowl. In a separate bowl, whisk the eggs for 30 seconds to 1 minute or until pale. Add the eggs to the dry ingredients, along with the pumpkin puree, coconut oil and maple syrup and mix thoroughly. Lastly, fold through the walnuts and cranberries.

Spoon the mixture into the loaf tin and smooth with the back of a spoon. Sprinkle with the pumpkin seeds and chia seeds. Bake for 35–40 minutes or until a skewer inserted into the middle comes out clean and the loaf is slightly browned on top. Leave in the tin for 5 minutes, then turn it out and allow to cool before slicing.

Serve 1–2 slices per person with sliced strawberries, drizzled with tahini and/or honey, if using.

BROCCOLI *and* PESTO FRITTATA

SERVES 4

SAVE LEFTOVERS for MON BREAKFAST

Broccoli is such a brilliant veggie, but too many people throw away the stalk and waste valuable nutrients. This recipe uses the whole lot, making the most of the nutritious stalk. You can use any kind of milk here, and feel free to throw in any other vegetables you might have in the fridge.

2 heads broccoli, cut into small florets, stalks trimmed and diced

1 cup cherry tomatoes, halved or quartered

6 organic eggs

3 tablespoons almond milk (or milk of your choice)

2 heaped tablespoons Kale and Almond Chilli Pesto (see page 194)

2 tablespoons pine nuts (optional)

Preheat the oven to 200°C.

Set a steamer over a saucepan of gently boiling water and steam the broccoli florets and stalks until just tender, about 4–5 minutes.

Transfer the steamed broccoli to an ovenproof frying pan and add the tomatoes, spreading them both evenly over the base.

Beat together the eggs, milk and pesto and pour the mixture over the top of the broccoli and tomatoes. Sprinkle with the pine nuts, if using. Place the frying pan over low–medium heat and cook for 10 minutes until the bottom is set, then transfer to the oven for 5–10 minutes until set and browned.

Remove from the oven and allow to cool slightly before serving. This frittata serves 4, so cover the remaining half and store it in the fridge for tomorrow's lunch.

SPICED CARROT *and* ORANGE JUICE

SERVES 2

If you don't have a juicer at home, you can just buy a cold-pressed juice, but make sure it has a good balance of fruit and vegetables. If you can't find fresh turmeric, stir in ½ teaspoon of ground turmeric to the juice instead.

1 orange, peeled

2½ large carrots, peeled

½ teaspoon ground turmeric or 1.5 cm piece of fresh turmeric, peeled

2.5 cm piece of ginger, peeled

½ lemon, flesh only

Place all the ingredients through a juicer and enjoy.

My favourite juice combo!

KIWI, AVOCADO *and* LIME SMOOTHIE BOWL

SERVES 2

Smoothie bowls are a different way to enjoy your regular morning smoothie. Pack in your greens, add some healthy fat, and nuts or seeds for extra protein, and then my favourite part – toppings!

1 cup kale leaves, stalks
 discarded, torn
½ avocado
1 kiwi fruit, peeled, plus extra
 slices to serve
1 tablespoon chia seeds
squeeze of lime juice
½–1 cup coconut water
4 tablespoons Homemade
 Muesli (see below)
4 strawberries, hulled and sliced

Place the kale, avocado, kiwi fruit, chia seeds, lime juice and coconut water in a high-speed blender and blend until thick and smooth.

Pour into bowls and top with the muesli, extra kiwi fruit and strawberries.

HOMEMADE MUESLI

MAKES 8 CUPS

This delicious homemade muesli will keep for up to 4 months but we'll be using it in other recipes!

2 cups rolled oats
2 cups spelt flakes
½ cup sunflower seeds
½ cup pumpkin seeds
1 cup roughly chopped raw
 almonds and walnuts
1 cup sultanas or 1 cup dried
 cranberries or ½ cup of each
1 cup coconut flakes
2 teaspoons ground cinnamon

Combine all the ingredients and store in an airtight container.

CHAI BIRCHER MUESLI

SERVES 2

Make this recipe the night before and keep it in the fridge overnight, allowing you to just grab and go in the morning.

1½ cups Homemade Muesli
(see page 142)
1¾ cups chai tea, made with
2 tea bags
1 green apple, ¾ grated,
¼ sliced
½ teaspoon ground cinnamon
¼ teaspoon ground cardamom
(optional)
¼ teaspoon ground ginger
(optional)
1 teaspoon honey
1 teaspoon pure vanilla extract
coconut yoghurt (or yoghurt of
your choice), to serve

Combine all the ingredients except the sliced apple in a small bowl or jar, then cover and leave overnight. Serve topped with the sliced apple and coconut yoghurt.

Extra chai tea bags can be used to brew some tea as a snack with some almond milk and honey.

EGG *and* HUMMUS *on* SOURDOUGH

SERVES 2

Avo on toast will always hold a special place in my heart, but I do love mixing up my flavours. Swapping avocado for hummus ramps up the protein content and, with your Homemade Hummus (see page 202) all ready to go in the fridge, this is an easy one to whip up. Hummus is a great alternative when ripe avocados are out of season and hard to come by. You can just toast the sourdough if you want to skip the char-grilling, and don't forget your Cucumber, Celery, Pineapple and Mint Juice (see below) for added greens!

2 organic eggs
2 large slices of sourdough
1 tablespoon extra virgin
   olive oil
2 heaped tablespoons
   Homemade Hummus
   (see page 202)
2 tablespoons pumpkin seeds
sea salt and freshly ground
   black pepper

Bring a saucepan of water to the boil, then reduce the heat to low. Carefully drop in the eggs and cook for 5–6 minutes (8 minutes if you like them hard-boiled). Remove from the saucepan and run under cool water for 30 seconds, then peel and cut in half.

Meanwhile, rub the sourdough on both sides with the olive oil and preheat a char-grill pan over medium heat. Char-grill until toasted and char-marks appear.

Spread the toast with hummus and place the eggs on top. Sprinkle over the pumpkin seeds then season with salt and pepper to serve.

CUCUMBER, CELERY, PINEAPPLE *and* MINT JUICE

SAVE
LEFTOVERS
for MON
BREAKFAST

SERVES 2

If you don't have a juicer, you can just buy a cold-pressed juice. Alternatively, grab your blender and swap the celery for a few handfuls of baby spinach, then add a cup of coconut water for a hydrating and alkalising smoothie.

4 Lebanese cucumbers
4 celery stalks, plus leaves
¼ pineapple, cut into four slices
4 sprigs mint, leaves picked

Place all the ingredients through a cold-pressed juicer and enjoy.

MANGO *and* COCONUT SMOOTHIE

SERVES 2

This creamy smoothie is super-hydrating thanks to the coconut water, making it perfect for a post-workout brekkie. Mango provides a delicious sweetness as well as a boost of prebiotic fibre for a healthy gut, antioxidants and vitamins A, C and E.

1 mango, peeled and deseeded
½ cup coconut flakes
1 frozen banana
2 tablespoons almond butter
2 tablespoons psyllium husk
3 cups coconut water

Place all the ingredients in a high-speed blender and blend until smooth.

Mango and coconut: the ultimate tropical combo!

BUCKWHEAT BLUEBERRY PANCAKES

SERVES 2

The best way to start your weekend! These pancakes are so easy to prepare – you simply throw all the ingredients into a food processor or blender and then pour out the batter. Blueberries are high in potassium, which is important for your muscles, and antioxidants, which neutralise those nasty free radicals. Plus, your taste buds will love the juicy surprises with each mouthful!

2 over-ripe bananas, mashed
2 organic eggs
¼ teaspoon baking powder
2 tablespoons buckwheat flour
I teaspoon ground cinnamon
I tablespoon coconut oil
or butter
⅓ cup blueberries, plus extra
to serve
2 heaped tablespoons coconut
yoghurt (or yoghurt of your
choice)
2 teaspoons honey or maple
syrup

Blend the bananas, eggs, baking powder, buckwheat flour and cinnamon in a food processor or high-speed blender until well combined. (Alternatively, whisk in a bowl until well combined.) Stir through the blueberries.

Heat the coconut oil or butter in a frying pan over low–medium heat and add 3 tablespoons of the mixture to the pan. Cook for I–2 minutes, then turn over and cook for a further I–2 minutes until cooked through. Keep warm in the oven while you cook the remaining batter to make about 6 small pancakes.

Serve the pancakes with coconut yoghurt, extra berries and honey or maple syrup.

GREENS *with* EGGS *and* CHILLI

SERVES 2

This is the perfect weekend fry-up and an irresistible way to start your day with plenty of nutrients. Not just a great source of protein, the egg yolk provides us with omega-3 fats, and vitamins A and D. It doesn't get much cleaner than greens and eggs, but you can serve it with a slice of sourdough toast if you wish.

- 1 tablespoon extra virgin olive oil
- 2 spring onions, finely chopped
- 2 cloves garlic, crushed
- 1 cup button mushrooms, finely sliced
- 8–10 kale leaves, stalks discarded, roughly torn
- 4 large handfuls of baby spinach
- juice of ½ lemon
- 4 organic eggs
- sea salt and freshly ground black pepper
- 1 handful of flat-leaf parsley leaves
- 1 long red chilli, deseeded if you like

Heat the olive oil in a frying pan over medium heat and saute the spring onion, garlic and mushrooms for 2 minutes.

Add the kale, spinach and lemon juice and saute for another 1–2 minutes.

Spread the greens to cover the base of the pan and then crack the eggs on top. Cook for 3–4 minutes, then place a lid on top for 1–2 minutes until the egg whites looks set but the yolks are still soft. (You can also put this under a preheated grill – if using an ovenproof frying pan – for a crisper finish if you prefer, but be sure not to put it too close to the heat as the greens will burn.)

Sprinkle over some salt and pepper, parsley and fresh chilli to serve.

PUMPKIN *and* ROSEMARY FRITTATAS

MAKES 12

These little pockets of flavour are a great option for us busy people! They don't take a lot of time to prepare and will keep in the fridge for up to 5 days, so you can grab and go whenever you need them. Feta is a tasty addition here for those who can tolerate dairy – distribute about ⅓ cup evenly among the muffin holes after the pumpkin.

1 tablespoon extra virgin olive oil, plus extra for greasing
½ small kent (jap) pumpkin, peeled
½ onion, diced
1 clove garlic, crushed
2 sprigs rosemary, leaves chopped
5 organic eggs, whisked
½ cup milk of your choice
sea salt and freshly ground black pepper

Preheat the oven to 180°C.

Grease 12 holes of a one-third cup capacity muffin tray with olive oil and line each hole with baking paper. Grate the pumpkin over a clean tea towel, then squeeze out as much liquid as possible. You will need 2 cups of grated pumpkin for this recipe.

Heat the olive oil in a frying pan over medium heat and saute the onion for 2 minutes, then add the garlic and rosemary, and fry for 1 minute. Add the grated pumpkin and cook for another 2–3 minutes until slightly softened.

Combine the egg and milk and season with salt and pepper.

Divide the pumpkin mixture evenly among the prepared muffin holes. Pour over the egg mixture evenly, giving it a bit of a stir to distribute the pumpkin. Bake for 15–20 minutes or until golden and set. Place on paper towel after baking to soak up any moisture on the bottom.

Reserve 6 frittatas for Wednesday's lunch and serve with 1 handful of mixed lettuce and ½ cup of cherry tomatoes.

APPLE *and* DATE BUCKWHEAT PORRIDGE *with* FIGS

SERVES 2

Buckwheat porridge is a tasty gluten-free alternative to traditional oats. The buckwheat is best digested when it has been soaked overnight; alternatively, you can buy activated buckwheat (buckinis), which doesn't need to be pre-soaked as it has already been cooked and dried. If figs aren't in season, use ½ cup of fresh or frozen mixed berries instead.

½ cup buckwheat groats, rinsed
1 tablespoon chia seeds
2 medjool dates, pitted
  and diced
½ teaspoon ground cinnamon
1 cup almond milk (or milk
  of your choice)
1 red apple, cored and grated
2 fresh figs, quartered
2 tablespoons raw almonds,
  roughly chopped
honey, to drizzle

Combine the buckwheat, chia seeds, dates, cinnamon and milk in a bowl and leave in the fridge overnight.

In the morning, transfer the buckwheat mixture to a small saucepan over low heat. Add 1 cup of water and the grated apple. Simmer, stirring regularly, for 8–10 minutes for a nice and thick consistency, 5 minutes if you prefer it less thick.

Top with the figs and almonds and drizzle with honey, to serve.

KIWI *and* GREENS SMOOTHIE

SERVES 2

Stacked with vitamin C and potassium, this green smoothie is the ultimate nourishing start to the day. Blending whole fruit retains the fibre content, which slows down the release of the natural sugars. Chia seeds will add some thickness (especially if you let the smoothie sit in the fridge for a little while) and are a good source of healthy fats too.

I handful of baby spinach
I handful of kale leaves, stalks discarded, torn
2 kiwi fruit
I frozen peeled banana
I tablespoon chia seeds
I cup freshly squeezed orange juice

Place all the ingredients and 2 cups of water in a high-speed blender and blend until smooth.

This recipe is like a childhood memory!

SPINACH *and* MUSHROOM FRY-UP *with* BOILED EGGS

SERVES 2

Soft-boiled eggs with toast soldiers for dipping into the runny yolk ... yum! In this grown-up version, the nutritional value is boosted by adding greens and mushrooms. And what's more, it ticks off all elements of a balanced meal: protein, slow-releasing carbohydrates, healthy fats and veggies.

4 organic eggs
1 tablespoon extra virgin
  olive oil
2 cups button mushrooms,
  halved
4 large handfuls of baby spinach
2 slices of sourdough toast,
  cut in half
1 teaspoon chilli flakes

Bring a saucepan of water to the boil, then reduce the heat to low. Carefully drop in the eggs and cook for 5–6 minutes (8 minutes if you like them hard-boiled), before cooling under running water. Peel and set aside.

Meanwhile, heat the olive oil in a frying pan over medium–high heat and saute the mushrooms for 3–4 minutes until tender. Add the spinach and cook for 1–2 minutes until wilted.

Divide the spinach and mushroom mixture between plates and top each one with two soft-boiled eggs. Sprinkle with chilli flakes and serve with the sourdough slices for dipping into the runny yolk!

BERRY *and* PASSIONFRUIT SMOOTHIE BOWL

SERVES 2

Just like a big bowl of berry ice-cream for breakfast – what a way to pack in your 2 serves of fruit for the day! I often add some protein powder to the mix too, which keeps me feeling fuller for longer. Because fruit is naturally higher in sugar than vegetables, I recommend you stick to veggie-based snacks for the rest of the day.

I heaped cup frozen mixed
berries
I frozen peeled banana
¼ cup milk of your choice
(coconut or almond
work well)
2 passionfruit, halved
coconut flakes, to serve
chopped raw almonds, to serve

Blend the berries, banana and milk in a high-speed blender until smooth (add a touch more milk if needed).

Pour into two bowls and top with the passionfruit, coconut flakes and almonds.

BANANA, ALMOND BUTTER *and* BERRY JAM *on* TOAST

SERVES 2

This breakfast tastes so indulgent but is full of healthy, nourishing ingredients! The chia seeds lend well to a jam because they absorb the liquid brilliantly, resulting in the perfect spreadable-jelly consistency. Store the leftover jam in the fridge for up to 2 weeks and enjoy on toast or rice cakes, or swirled into yoghurt. It will also freeze well for up to 3 months.

1 tablespoon olive oil or butter
1 banana, sliced in half lengthways
2 slices of sourdough or leftover Pumpkin and Cranberry Loaf (see page 138), toasted
2 tablespoons almond butter

BERRY JAM (Makes 1½–2 cups)
3 tablespoons chia seeds
½ cup freshly squeezed orange juice
1 cup fresh mixed berries
2 tablespoons maple syrup
1 tablespoon freshly squeezed lemon juice

To make the berry jam, combine the chia seeds and orange juice in a bowl and leave for 10 minutes. Place the berries in a food processor and blend to a puree, then transfer to a saucepan with the chia mixture and maple syrup. Simmer for 10 minutes over low heat, stirring regularly, until thickened. Add the lemon juice and remove the pan from the heat.

Meanwhile, heat the oil or butter in a frying pan over medium heat and add the banana, cut-side down. Cook for 3–4 minutes until browned and caramelised.

Spread the toast with almond butter and 1 tablespoon of berry jam, and serve topped with the caramelised banana.

GREEN PESTO OMELETTE

SERVES 2

An omelette is the perfect weekend breakfast and such a good way to get a head start on your vegetable intake for the day. Cafes often use lots of cream and butter to achieve that super-silky texture, so making yours at home is the best option for keeping it clean.

1 zucchini, grated
sea salt
2 tablespoons Kale and Almond Chilli Pesto (see page 194)
4 organic eggs
2 tablespoons extra virgin olive oil
4 kale leaves, stalks discarded, finely chopped
½ long red chilli, sliced and deseeded if you like

Remove the pesto from the fridge and let it soften for a few minutes while you prepare the other ingredients.

Grate the zucchini over a clean tea towel, spread thinly and sprinkle with salt. Leave to sit for 5 minutes before squeezing out as much liquid as possible.

Whisk 2 of the eggs in a bowl and stir through 1 tablespoon of pesto. Heat half the olive oil in a frying pan over low–medium heat and pour in the egg and pesto mixture to cover the base of the pan. When the egg is beginning to bubble on the surface, add half of the zucchini and kale and fold over the omelette. Cook for 1–2 minutes until cooked to your liking.

Repeat with the remaining olive oil, eggs, pesto and veggies to make the second omelette. Top with fresh chilli to serve.

Get creative!

Weekend omelettes are one of the best ways to use up leftover veg from the week. Throw in some mushrooms, diced capsicum or tomatoes, and fresh herbs such as flat-leaf parsley or chives, and top with crumbled goat's cheese, black sesame seeds or rocket leaves. The possibilities are endless and you can't go wrong!

PEAR *and* BLUEBERRY SMOOTHIE

SERVES 2

Smoothies can be a healthy (and easy) breakfast option, but it's important to get the balance of nutrients right because many recipes call for *a lot* of fruit. Balancing the natural sugars in the fruit with some veg and a scoop of protein powder helps control blood-sugar levels. If protein powder isn't your thing, you can add 2 tablespoons of chia seeds, which, along with the cashews, will provide some protein. You'll be using lettuce cups for dinner tonight so take off any good 'cup' leaves and put aside for tonight, then use the rest for this smoothie.

I pear, cored
½ cup fresh or frozen
  blueberries
½ cup shredded iceberg lettuce
⅓ cup raw cashews
I scoop of protein powder
½ teaspoon ground cinnamon
I cup coconut milk (or milk of
  your choice)

Place all the ingredients and 2 cups of water in a high-speed blender and blend until smooth.

COCONUT YOGHURT *with* MUESLI *and* PASSIONFRUIT

SERVES 2

This is such a speedy breakfast to whip up when you've already made the Homemade Muesli in Week 1. Both coconut yoghurt and muesli are quite energy- (and nutrient-) dense so small portions will go a long way. Add some fresh berries for a hit of fibre, and passionfruit for vitamins C and A.

½ cup coconut yoghurt
   (or yoghurt of your choice)
½ cup Homemade Muesli
   (see page 142)
½ cup fresh mixed berries
2 passionfruit, cut in half

Serve the coconut yoghurt in small bowls, topped with the muesli, berries and passionfruit.

Winter fruit alternatives

Summer fruits such as passionfruit can be hard to come by, or expensive, when they're out of season. In the winter months, stewed fruit such as rhubarb can be a great alternative to fresh berries. Simply grab a bunch of rhubarb, trim the stems and discard the leaves, then slice into 10 cm lengths. Place in a saucepan with ½ cup of water and 1 tablespoon of maple syrup or honey. Simmer over low heat for 5 minutes or until the water has evaporated and the rhubarb is soft. It will keep in the fridge for a week; it's a perfect addition to your morning muesli or chia pudding, and great as a topping for your Pumpkin and Cranberry Loaf (see page 138), along with some nut butter.

COCONUT SCRAMBLED EGGS
with ASPARAGUS *on* TOAST

SERVES 2

The key to cooking good scrambled eggs is to keep the temperature low and gently fold the eggs over themselves. The nutritional value here is bolstered with spinach and some roasted asparagus, which is high in immune-boosting antioxidants as well as potassium, folic acid and vitamin C.

1 bunch asparagus, trimmed
sea salt and freshly ground
   black pepper
2 tablespoons extra virgin
   olive oil
4 organic eggs
2 tablespoons coconut milk
   (or milk of your choice)
pinch of chilli flakes
2 large handfuls of baby spinach
2 slices of sourdough toast

Preheat the oven to 180°C.

Lay the asparagus spears on a baking tray, sprinkle with salt and pepper and drizzle with 1 tablespoon of the olive oil. Roast for 10 minutes or until tender.

Meanwhile, whisk the eggs together with the milk until pale. Add the chilli flakes and a pinch of salt and pepper. Heat a frying pan over low heat and add the remaining olive oil. Pour in the egg mixture and place the spinach on top. Regularly and gently fold the eggs and spinach over themselves, until the egg starts to set but is still soft and the spinach wilts, about 5 minutes.

Serve the eggs on the sourdough toast with the roast asparagus on the side.

GREEN FRUIT SALAD *with* CASHEW CREAM

SERVES 2

Fruit salad and yoghurt is a very popular breakfast; however, I want to share with you my dairy-free alternative: cashew cream! Cashews are a good source of magnesium, phosphorus, iron and potassium and provide a small amount of protein too. I suggest soaking them overnight so in the morning you can just blitz all the ingredients together and you're good to go. You can of course use your favourite yoghurt instead if you prefer – just ensure you are keeping an eye on those labels, opting only for ingredients you recognise and a low sugar content.

I kiwi fruit, diced (remove the skin if you like)
I handful of green grapes, halved
I green apple, cored and diced
½ pomegranate, seeds only
2 tablespoons finely chopped mint
½ cup Cashew Cream (see below)

Combine the fruit and serve topped with mint and ½ cup of the cashew cream.

CASHEW CREAM

MAKES ABOUT 1½ CUPS

I cup raw cashews
2 tablespoons freshly squeezed lemon juice
I teaspoon pure vanilla extract
I tablespoon maple syrup
¼–½ cup warm water

To make the cashew cream, place the cashews in a shallow bowl with enough water to cover. Cover and soak at room temperature for at least 2 hours, ideally overnight.

Drain well, then place the soaked cashews in a food processor or high-speed blender with the lemon juice, vanilla, maple syrup and warm water and blend until creamy (start with 3 tablespoons of water and add more as needed to achieve a smooth consistency).

Store the cashew cream in the fridge for up to 6 days. (Keep 4 heaped tablespoons aside for other recipes in the meal plan and the rest can be used as snacks with veggie sticks, berries or on toast/muffins!)

A squeeze of lemon juice on your green fruits will stop them from browning if you're making this ahead of time.

PRE-WORKOUT SMOOTHIE

SERVES 2

This is an ideal smoothie for some pre-workout fuel. Caffeine has been shown to increase performance so this is the perfect time to enjoy it. However, long-term caffeine use and multiple servings per day can be detrimental to your nervous system and adrenals, so just be sure not to rely on it for energy.

1 frozen peeled banana
1 teaspoon honey
1 tablespoon raw cacao powder
1 shot (30 ml) of espresso
  (optional)
2 tablespoons walnuts
1 cup coconut milk (or milk of
  your choice)

Place all the ingredients and 2 cups of water in a high-speed blender and blend until smooth.

Simply omit the espresso if you're not a coffee fan.

SMOKED SALMON EGG MUFFINS
with ROAST TOMATOES

SERVES 2

Defrost the wraps you have left over from Week 2 and get ready for a deliciously flavoursome breakfast! Smoked salmon is another easy way to incorporate those important omega-3 fats and protein into your diet. Adding a bed of rocket delivers bitter properties that stimulate enzyme production and help with digestion.

extra virgin olive oil,
   for greasing
3 wholegrain wraps
4 organic eggs
3 tablespoons milk of your
   choice
pinch of chilli flakes
sea salt and freshly ground
   black pepper
100 g smoked salmon, chopped
2 tablespoons chopped
   flat-leaf parsley
12 cherry tomatoes on the vine
2 handfuls of rocket

Preheat the oven to 180°C and grease six holes of a ⅓ cup capacity muffin tray with olive oil.

Encase the wraps in foil and place in the oven until warm and soft, about 5–10 minutes. Cut each wrap in half. Whisk the eggs and milk together with the chilli flakes and a pinch of salt and pepper.

Line each muffin hole with a wrap half to make a cup shape (this is a bit fiddly but they don't have to be perfect). Divide the smoked salmon and parsley between the wrap cases and then pour in the egg mixture.

Place the tomatoes (still on the vine) on a baking tray.

Cook the tomatoes and muffins for 15–20 minutes until the muffins are set (cover with foil if the edges are browning too much). Serve 3 muffins per person with the roast tomatoes and rocket.

AVOCADO *on* TOAST *with* CASHEW CREAM *and* PASSIONFRUIT

SERVES 2

This might sound like a strange combination, but I promise the crunch of the toast with the creaminess of the cashew cream and avocado, and the sweetness of the passionfruit sauce is seriously good! It's also full of healthy fats and slow-releasing carbohydrates.

2 passionfruit
1 teaspoon honey
juice of ¼ lime
2 slices of sourdough toast
2 heaped tablespoons Cashew
   Cream (see page 174)
½ avocado, sliced

Place the passionfruit pulp in a saucepan with the honey, lime juice and 2 tablespoons of water. Simmer over low heat until the mixture thickens slightly, about 2–3 minutes.

Spread the sourdough toast with cashew cream, top with avocado slices and drizzle with the passionfruit sauce.

COCONUT, CHIA and MANGO PARFAIT

SERVES 2

Fly out the door in the morning with a nourishing and satisfying breakfast on hand, thanks to these make-ahead parfaits. Chia seeds top us up with fibre, protein and omega-3s, and are a great source of B vitamins to support our metabolism, while cinnamon can help to balance out our blood-sugar levels.

⅔ cup chia seeds
2 cups coconut milk
⅓ cup honey
I teaspoon ground cinnamon
I large mango
I tablespoon chopped mixed nuts and/or coconut flakes

Combine the chia seeds, coconut milk, honey and cinnamon in a bowl and place in the fridge to thicken overnight.

Slice your mango into small cubes (see opposite). Spoon half of the chia mixture into the bottom of two jars and add a quarter of the mango cubes to each jar. Top with the remaining chia mixture, before adding the remaining mango. Chill in the fridge until ready to eat, then sprinkle over the nuts and/or coconut flakes to serve.

How to cut
MANGO

One of the best things about summer is my favourite fruit coming into season – mangoes! They have an unusual shaped pit in the centre that can be hard to cut around. Here's how to get perfect cubes!

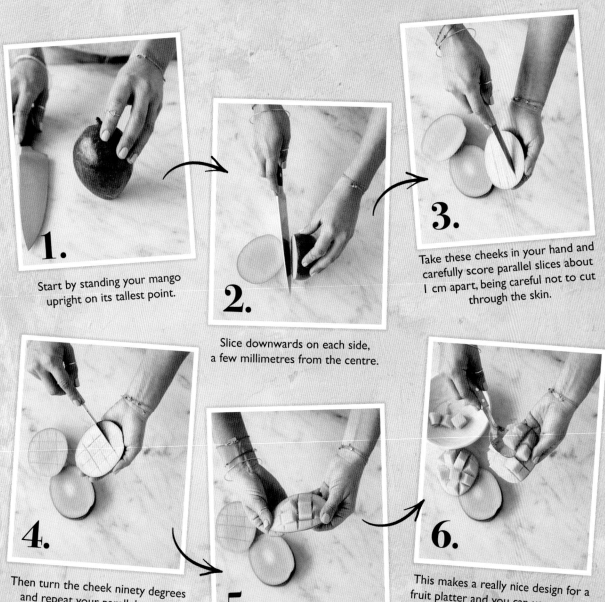

1. Start by standing your mango upright on its tallest point.

2. Slice downwards on each side, a few millimetres from the centre.

3. Take these cheeks in your hand and carefully score parallel slices about 1 cm apart, being careful not to cut through the skin.

4. Then turn the cheek ninety degrees and repeat your parallel cuts to make a checkerboard pattern.

5. Press up on the skin in the centre to invert, and your cubes should pop outward.

6. This makes a really nice design for a fruit platter and you can use a spoon to scoop the fruit out from here.

PROTEIN PANCAKES

SERVES 2

Just four ingredients are all you need to whip up these nutritionally balanced and delicious pancakes! The consistency of protein powders can vary, so you may like to make a small test pancake to check it doesn't get too dry. If it does, add a splash of coconut water to your batter.

2 ripe bananas
2 organic eggs
2 scoops of protein powder
   (optional)
1 teaspoon ground cinnamon
½ cup toasted coconut chips
   (optional)
1 cup coconut yoghurt
   (or yoghurt of your choice)
1 cup fresh or frozen
   mixed berries
2 tablespoons maple syrup

Mash the bananas in a large bowl using a fork. Add the eggs, protein powder (if using) and cinnamon and mix well.

Heat a small, non-stick frying pan over low heat and pour in ⅓ cup of batter. (If you don't have a non-stick frying pan, use ½ teaspoon of coconut oil or a coconut oil spray to grease the pan.) Cook for 3–4 minutes until the pancake is browned underneath and the batter on top holds in place. Flip and cook for 1 minute on the other side or until just browned. Repeat to make the remaining pancakes. This makes 4 large or 6 small pancakes.

Serve with coconut chips (if using), yoghurt and berries scattered on top, and a drizzle of maple syrup.

If you are using frozen berries, toss them around in the pan after you've finished the pancakes for a few minutes to thaw before serving.

MINT CHOC CHIP SMOOTHIE

SERVES 2

A nourishing alternative to old-school ice-cream! The avocado and banana in this recipe make for a super-creamy consistency while the coconut water is hydrating and refreshing.

1 frozen peeled banana
1 cup coconut water
¼ avocado
1 sprig mint, leaves torn, plus
   extra for topping
1 handful of baby spinach
½ cup cacao nibs, plus extra
   for topping

Place all the ingredients in a high-speed blender and blend until combined.

Top with extra cacao nibs and mint leaves.

WARMING CINNAMON
and CHIA SEED PORRIDGE

SERVES 2

The kind of winter brekkie that warms the soul! Adding chia seeds to the oats gives us a boost of omega-3 fatty acids. The carbohydrate, protein and fibre in this porridge is the perfect way to refuel your muscles after morning training. It's quick to throw together and will keep you full of energy all morning.

1 cup rolled oats
⅓ cup chia seeds
pinch of sea salt
1 teaspoon ground cinnamon
2 tablespoons honey, plus extra to serve
1 cup mixed berries and/or mixed nuts
toasted coconut chips, to serve

Place the oats, chia seeds and 3 cups of water in a bowl and leave to soak in the fridge overnight.

In the morning, transfer the soaked oats and chia seeds to a saucepan and add the salt, cinnamon and 1½ cups of water. Place over high heat and bring to the boil, then reduce the heat to medium. Simmer for 6–7 minutes, stirring, until thick and creamy, then remove from the heat. Allow to stand for 4–5 minutes to cool and thicken further. (If you like a thicker porridge, you can heat it for a bit longer; if you prefer a runnier porridge simply add some more water.)

Pour the porridge into bowls and drizzle with honey. Top with berries and/or mixed nuts and toasted coconut chips, to serve.

OVERNIGHT APPLE CRUMBLE BIRCHER MUESLI

SERVES 2

This breakfast is full of such epic comforting flavours you might want to have it for dessert! The sweet and spicy combination takes cues from a traditional crumble, but my version is full of fibre and perfectly balanced by the tartness of a granny smith apple. Equally delicious hot or cold: take your pick.

I cup rolled oats

2 cups almond milk (or milk of your choice)

I tablespoon raisins

2 tablespoons honey

I teaspoon ground cinnamon

I granny smith apple, peeled, cored and grated

½ cup unsalted mixed nuts (your choice – almonds, cashews, etc) or coconut chips

I tablespoon yoghurt of your choice (optional)

Combine the oats, milk, raisins, honey, cinnamon and grated apple in a bowl. Refrigerate overnight to allow all the flavours to infuse.

To serve warm, heat the oat mixture in a saucepan over medium–high heat for 10 minutes, stirring constantly and adding a little extra milk or water if necessary. Alternatively, you can microwave on high for 30 seconds.

Scatter over your favourite nuts or coconut chips and a drizzle of honey, to serve.

Toasting nuts

To toast your nuts for a little extra crunch, chop them roughly, and place them in a frying pan over medium–high heat. Stir frequently for about 3 minutes as they toast. When they are golden brown, remove from the heat. If making ahead, store in an airtight container until ready to serve.

QUINOA POWER BREKKIE

SERVES 2

There's absolutely no messing around with the goodness in here. Quinoa is an awesome gluten-free addition to your breakfast repertoire as it's a complete protein and a wonderful source of fibre. The eggs will bulk up the protein quota to keep you full all morning, and along with the linseeds are a great source of omega-3. Kale, like all dark leafy greens, assists with detoxification and building healthy bones and skin, thanks to a host of essential vitamins. This brekkie is also a great make-ahead option as it reheats well in the microwave or on the stovetop.

But any colour will work! ↗

- 1 cup tricolour quinoa
- 2 tablespoons coconut oil
- 1 onion, finely diced
- 4 kale leaves, stalks discarded
- 1 cup cherry tomatoes, halved
- 1 long red chilli, deseeded and finely chopped
- 3 organic eggs
- sea salt and freshly ground black pepper
- 1 tablespoon linseeds

Rinse the quinoa well and place it in a saucepan with 2 cups of water. Bring to the boil, then reduce the heat to low and simmer until the water has been absorbed and the quinoa 'tails' appear, about 12–15 minutes. Remove from the heat and set aside, with the lid on, for 5 minutes, then fluff with a fork.

Melt the coconut oil in a large frying pan over medium heat and gently fry the onion for 1–2 minutes to soften. Massage the kale in your hands, then tear it roughly and add to the pan. Add the cherry tomatoes and chilli to the pan and toss through. Cook for 2–3 minutes to allow the kale leaves to turn a deep vibrant green and soften.

Whisk the eggs together with 2 tablespoons of water.

Reduce the heat to low and shift the vegetables to one side. Pour in the egg and fold gently through the vegetables as it cooks. Season with salt and pepper.

Remove the pan from the heat and fold the cooked quinoa through the vegetables. Serve immediately, topped with linseeds, or allow to cool and refrigerate if making ahead.

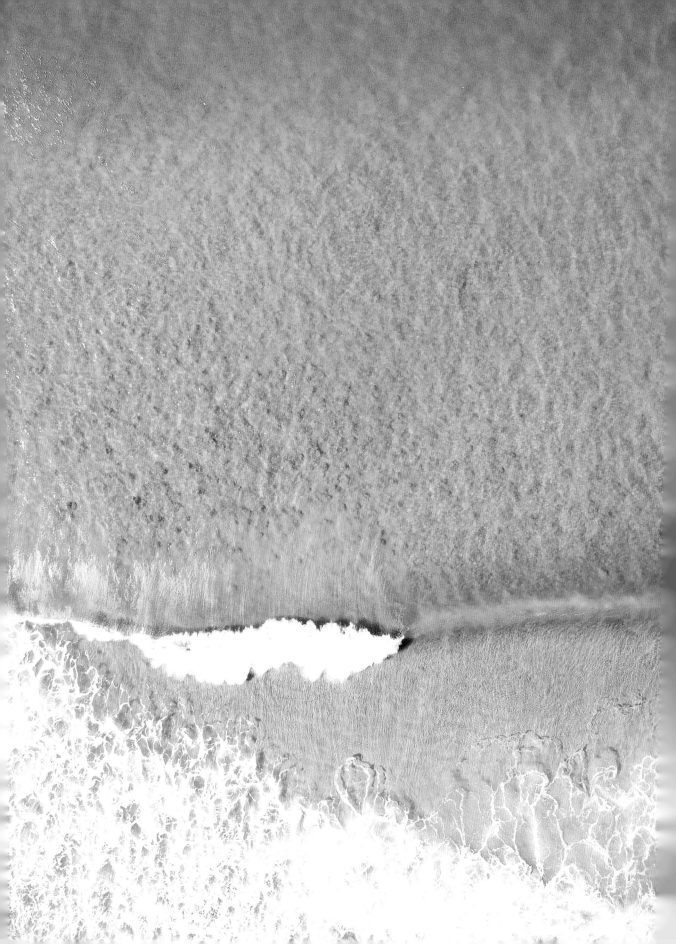

Lunch

CHICKEN, AVOCADO *and* BLUEBERRY SALAD

SERVES 2

I love adding fruit to my salads for a surprise hit of sweetness. This recipe is a simple but powerful combination of protein from the chicken (to help keep us feeling full), healthy fats from the avocado, antioxidants from the blueberries, and a stack of vitamins and minerals from the spinach. If you're making this ahead of time, keep the dressing separate and just pour it over when serving.

2 tablespoons pumpkin seeds
4 chicken tenderloins
   (about 200 g in total)
sea salt and freshly ground
   black pepper
1 tablespoon extra virgin
   olive oil
½ avocado, sliced
½ cup blueberries
2 celery stalks, finely sliced
2 cups baby spinach

DRESSING

1½ tablespoons extra virgin
   olive oil or macadamia oil
2 teaspoons balsamic vinegar
1 teaspoon honey
1 teaspoon dijon mustard
pinch of sea salt and freshly
   ground black pepper

To make the dressing, combine all the ingredients in a small bowl and mix well.

Place a frying pan over low heat and toast the pumpkin seeds until starting to pop and slightly brown, about 2–4 minutes. Tip the toasted pumpkin seeds into a bowl and set aside.

Season the chicken with salt and pepper. Add the olive oil to the pan and place over medium–high heat. Cook the tenderloins for 2–3 minutes on each side, until cooked through. Leave to cool for a few minutes, then slice.

Arrange the avocado, blueberries, celery, spinach and pumpkin seeds in two bowls. Drizzle over the dressing and top with the chicken.

PESTO TUNA SALAD

SERVES 2

Pan-fried fresh tuna and tinned tuna both work really well in this meal. Quinoa is an awesome pantry staple as it is a top source of protein, carbohydrate and fibre. Get ahead of your game by making this salad the night before and just stir through the pesto when serving to ensure the lettuce stays crisp.

½ cup white quinoa
200 g tuna steak or 2 × 95 g tins tuna in olive oil, drained
½ head broccoli, cut into florets, stalk trimmed and diced
½ iceberg lettuce, shredded
2 tablespoons dried cranberries
3 tablespoons raw almonds, chopped
2 tablespoons goat's cheese (optional)
2 heaped tablespoons Kale and Almond Chilli Pesto (see below)

Rinse the quinoa well and place it in a saucepan with ¾ cup of water. Bring to the boil, then reduce the heat to low and simmer until the water has been absorbed and the quinoa 'tails' appear, about 12–15 minutes. Remove from the heat and set aside, with the lid on, for 5 minutes, then fluff with a fork.

Meanwhile, if you are using fresh tuna, heat a small frying pan over medium–high heat and sear the tuna for 1–2 minutes on each side (longer if you prefer it well done).

Set a steamer over a saucepan of simmering water. Place the broccoli in the steamer and lightly steam until just tender, about 4–5 minutes, then rinse under cold water.

Combine the quinoa, broccoli, lettuce, tuna, cranberries and almonds in a bowl and crumble over the goat's cheese (if using). Stir through the pesto just before serving.

KALE *and* ALMOND CHILLI PESTO

MAKES ABOUT 2 CUPS

Make a jar of pesto for the fridge, so it's easy to whip out and take the flavour of your meal up a notch.

4 cloves garlic, peeled
½ cup raw almonds
1 cup pumpkin seeds
4 large handfuls of kale leaves, stalks discarded, roughly torn
½ cup basil leaves
2 tablespoons freshly squeezed lemon juice
½ long green chilli, deseeded if you like
½ teaspoon sea salt
½ teaspoon freshly ground black pepper
½ cup extra virgin olive oil

Place the garlic in a food processor or high-speed blender and blend to mince it up a bit. Add all the remaining ingredients, except the olive oil, and puree until the mixture is almost smooth. Slowly drizzle in the olive oil until your desired consistency is achieved.

Keep 2 tablespoons of the pesto in the freezer (in ice-cube trays) for Week 1 Sunday dinner and for Week 3.

Pesto is such a tasty addition to any dish.

QUINOA *with* SESAME SOFT-BOILED EGGS

SERVES 2

Power through your day with the multiple protein sources in this recipe – quinoa, eggs and edamame. You can buy frozen edamame (in their pods or shelled) at some supermarkets and Asian grocery stores. Simply thaw them in hot water and throw them in. I've added broccoli and snowpeas here too for extra nutrients and a flavour boost from chilli, ginger and garlic.

½ **cup white quinoa**

4 **organic eggs**

2 **tablespoons sesame seeds**

2 **teaspoons coconut oil**

½ **head broccoli, cut into florets, stalk trimmed and diced**

2 **cloves garlic, finely sliced**

1 **tablespoon finely chopped fresh ginger**

1 **long red chilli, sliced and deseeded if you like**

1 **large handful of snowpeas, trimmed and finely shredded**

⅓ **cup edamame beans, thawed and podded**

2 **spring onions, finely chopped**

Rinse the quinoa well and place it in a saucepan with ¾ cup of water. Bring to the boil, then reduce the heat to low and simmer until the water has been absorbed and the quinoa 'tails' appear, 12–15 minutes. Remove from the heat and set aside, with the lid on, for 5 minutes, then fluff with a fork.

Meanwhile, bring a saucepan of water to the boil, then reduce the heat to low. Carefully drop in the eggs and cook for 5–6 minutes (8 minutes if you like them hard-boiled), before cooling under running water. Peel the eggs and roll them in the sesame seeds (brush the eggs with a little oil if the sesame seeds don't want to stick). Halve the eggs then set aside.

Heat the coconut oil in a wok over medium–high heat, then add the broccoli and stir-fry for 2–3 minutes. Add the garlic, ginger and chilli, and stir-fry for a further minute. Add the quinoa, snowpeas and edamame, and stir-fry for a final 2 minutes.

Serve topped with the sesame eggs and spring onion.

ROASTED VEGGIE SALAD
with CRUNCHY CHICKPEAS

SERVES 2

Roasting is the perfect way to cook your veggies on a weekend, leaving you plenty of time to do other things you love! This recipe features root vegetables, which are nourishing and grounding, and chickpeas, an excellent source of protein and fibre.

1 × 400 g tin chickpeas, drained and rinsed
3 tablespoons extra virgin olive oil
sea salt and freshly ground black pepper
½ small (about 140 g) butternut pumpkin, peeled and cut into large chunks
1 parsnip, peeled and cut into 3 cm cubes
1 large carrot, peeled and cut into 3 cm chunks
2 sprigs rosemary
1 red onion, cut into wedges
½ cauliflower, cut into florets
1 zucchini, cut into 1 cm slices
1 eggplant, cut into 2 cm cubes
2 tablespoons goat's cheese (optional)

Preheat the oven to 180°C and line two baking trays with baking paper.

Place the chickpeas on one baking tray, rub with 1 tablespoon of the olive oil and sprinkle with salt and pepper. Place the pumpkin, parsnip and carrot on the other tray, rub with the remaining olive oil, sprinkle with salt and pepper and scatter with the rosemary sprigs.

Roast for 15 minutes, then add the remaining veggies to the pumpkin, parsnip and carrot, mixing gently to coat in the oil and seasoning.

Roast for a further 20–25 minutes until the veggies are tender and the chickpeas are crunchy.

Plate up the veggies, add the crunchy chickpeas and top with goat's cheese, if using.

These crunchy chickpeas are also great for snacks! Make them in bulk and store in an airtight container for up to 4 days.

BUCKWHEAT, STRAWBERRY *and* BASIL SALAD

SERVES 4

Lentils are a great vegetarian source of protein. Here their earthy flavour is balanced with the sweetness of juicy pomegranate and strawberries, which, along with the spinach, provide us with the vitamin C we need to stay fighting fit. Top it all off with an extra hit of protein and healthy fats from the walnuts and you have a nutrient-packed salad that's super-easy to throw together so you can head out and make the most of your weekend! The recipe makes 4 servings so you can enjoy the leftovers for lunch tomorrow.

1 cup buckwheat groats, rinsed
1 × 400 g tin brown lentils, drained and rinsed
4 large handfuls of baby spinach
1 Lebanese cucumber, thinly sliced
1 cup strawberries, hulled and quartered
½ pomegranate, seeds only
½ cup walnuts, chopped
1 handful of basil leaves

DRESSING
3 tablespoons extra virgin olive oil
1 tablespoon balsamic vinegar
1 tablespoon freshly squeezed lemon juice
sea salt and freshly ground black pepper

To make the dressing, combine all the ingredients in a bowl and mix well.

Place the buckwheat in a saucepan with 2 cups of water and bring to the boil. Reduce the heat, cover and simmer for 15–20 minutes until the water has been absorbed. Remove from the heat and set aside, with the lid on, for 5 minutes, then fluff with a fork.

Combine the buckwheat, lentils, spinach, cucumber, strawberries, pomegranate seeds, walnuts and basil. Serve into bowls, reserving half for lunch tomorrow. Drizzle over the dressing when you're ready to eat.

ZUCCHINI NOODLES *with* ROCKET, SALMON *and* HUMMUS

SERVES 2

Finding new and creative ways to eat your vegetables is one of the keys to enjoying amazing nutrition. Zucchini pasta is a lighter alternative to the regular kind and blends perfectly with the richness of salmon in this dish. Hummus makes an unbelievable creamy sauce, so is fantastic for anyone with a lactose intolerance like me!

2 large zucchini, spiralised (see page 253)
2 salmon fillets (about 200 g in total), cut into 2 cm pieces, or 2 × 95 g tins salmon, drained
2 handfuls of rocket
1 handful of flat-leaf parsley leaves
juice of ½ lemon
3 tablespoons Homemade Hummus (see below)

Set a steamer over a saucepan of simmering water. Place the zucchini noodles and fresh salmon, if using, in the steamer and lightly steam until just tender, about 1–2 minutes. Reserve 2 tablespoons of the cooking liquid.

Transfer the zucchini and salmon (add the tinned salmon here, if using) to a large saucepan over low heat. Add the reserved cooking liquid, rocket, parsley and lemon juice. Stir until well combined, then divide the hummus between serving plates and serve the noodle mixture on top.

HOMEMADE HUMMUS

MAKES 1½ CUPS

1 × 400 g tin chickpeas, drained and rinsed
1 teaspoon ground cumin
1 tablespoon tahini
juice of ½ lemon
good pinch of sea salt and freshly ground black pepper
⅓ cup olive oil, plus more if needed

To make the hummus, combine all the ingredients, apart from the olive oil, in a food processor. Slowly add the olive oil while the motor is running, until a smooth consistency is achieved (add more oil or a dash of water to reach a smoother consistency if needed). The hummus will keep in the fridge for 4–5 days.

TUNA, AVO *and* CHILLI SMASH *with* RAINBOW VEGGIES

SERVES 2

Why not get outside and enjoy some fresh air with this vibrant veggie platter. The tuna and avocado will provide healthy fats and protein to keep you going all afternoon.

¾ avocado
2 × 95 g tins tuna in olive oil,
  drained
juice of ½ lemon
pinch of chilli flakes
sea salt and freshly ground
  black pepper
½ red capsicum, cut into
  long strips
4 radishes, trimmed
1 Lebanese cucumber,
  cut into sticks
2 carrots, peeled and cut
  into sticks
½ lemon, cut into wedges

Mash the avocado, tuna, lemon juice, chilli and a pinch of salt and pepper together in a bowl.

Serve with the raw veggies for dipping and add a squeeze of lemon juice.

Just made for a picnic lunch!

CREAMY CHICKEN *and* SPINACH WRAP

SERVES 2

Wraps are a great option for a weekend picnic as they can be made in advance: just roll them up in baking paper and secure with twine or a toothpick until you're ready to eat. Shop smart when choosing your brand of wraps and look for a wholegrain option with minimal ingredients , and only ones that you recognise. Freeze the remaining wraps – we'll use them up in Week 4.

1 chicken breast (about 400 g), sliced into quarters
½ avocado
1 small handful of basil leaves
1 small handful of flat-leaf parsley leaves
2 tablespoons extra virgin olive oil
juice of ¼ lemon
sea salt and freshly ground black pepper
2 wholegrain wraps (20–25 cm)
2 handfuls of baby spinach
1 carrot, peeled and grated
¼ small red onion, diced
2 tablespoons chopped walnuts

Bring a saucepan of water to the boil, then reduce the heat to a simmer, add the chicken and poach for 5 minutes or until cooked through. Remove the chicken from the saucepan and leave to cool slightly, then finely chop.

Meanwhile, place the avocado, basil, parsley, olive oil, lemon juice, salt and pepper in a food processor and blitz until smooth (or chop the herbs very finely and mash all the ingredients in a small bowl).

Spread some avocado dressing on each wrap and divide the spinach and carrot between the two wraps. Place the chicken in a bowl with the onion and walnuts and combine well.

Place the chicken mixture in the centre of each wrap with a little of the remaining avocado dressing. Fold over one end, roll up tightly and enjoy!

SPICY FISH TACOS

SERVES 2

These spicy fish tacos don't get much easier, or much tastier! The lettuce cups make them light and gluten free but you could replace them with corn or wholegrain tortillas if you prefer. I love the spice from the jalapeno in this recipe, but feel free to discard the seeds if you don't like yours too hot!

2 teaspoons smoked paprika
½ teaspoon chilli flakes
200 g flathead tails or firm white fish fillets, cut into strips
2 tablespoons extra virgin olive oil
sea salt and freshly ground black pepper
1 corn cob, husk removed
⅛ red cabbage, shredded
2 radishes, trimmed and finely sliced
1 handful of coriander leaves, finely chopped
juice of ½ lime
4 large cos lettuce leaves

DRESSING
2 tablespoons coconut yoghurt (or yoghurt of your choice)
juice of ½ lime
½ jalapeno chilli, finely diced

On a plate, sprinkle the paprika and chilli flakes over the fish and add 1 tablespoon of the olive oil. Season with salt and pepper and turn to coat the fish well in the spices. Leave in the fridge while you prepare the salad.

Set a steamer over a saucepan of simmering water. Place the corn cob in the steamer and lightly steam until just tender, about 2–3 minutes. Cool the corn under running water, then cut off the kernels.

Combine the corn, cabbage, radish and coriander in a bowl. Add the remaining olive oil and the lime juice.

To make the dressing, combine the ingredients in a small bowl and mix well.

Heat a frying pan over medium–high heat and sear the fish for 1–2 minutes on each side or until just cooked through.

Serve the salad in the lettuce cups, topped with the fish and the coconut yoghurt dressing.

QUINOA, SWEET POTATO *and* APPLE SALAD

SERVES 2

Not only is quinoa a fantastic source of wholegrain fibre, it is a complete protein, which makes it a great option for vegetarian salads. Sweet potatoes with their bright orange flesh are rich in vitamin C and this also helps us absorb the iron from our leafy greens. To top it all off, throw in some avocado and walnuts for a boost of healthy fats, which promote brain health!

- 1 sweet potato, peeled and cut into small cubes
- 1 tablespoon extra virgin olive oil
- ½ cup quinoa
- 1 teaspoon fennel seeds (optional)
- 1 red apple, cut into matchsticks
- ½ red onion, thinly sliced
- 4 large handfuls of baby spinach
- ½ avocado, halved
- 1 tablespoon currants
- ⅓ cup walnuts
- 2 tablespoons sesame seeds
- 1 small handful of flat-leaf parsley leaves

DRESSING
- 1½ tablespoons extra virgin olive oil
- 2 teaspoons apple cider vinegar
- juice of ¼ lemon
- 1 teaspoon honey
- sea salt and freshly ground black pepper

Preheat the oven to 200°C and line a baking tray with baking paper.

Place the sweet potato on the prepared tray, drizzle with the olive oil and roast in the oven for 20–30 minutes, tossing halfway through cooking, until tender.

Rinse the quinoa well and place it in a saucepan with 1 cup of water and the fennel seeds, if using. Bring to the boil, then reduce the heat to medium and simmer, covered, until the water has been absorbed and the quinoa 'tails' appear, about 12–15 minutes. Remove from the heat and set aside, with the lid on, for 5 minutes, then fluff with a fork.

To make the dressing, combine all the ingredients in a bowl and mix well.

In a large bowl, combine the sweet potato and quinoa with all the remaining ingredients and pour over the dressing.

FRIED BROWN RICE *with* FISH

SERVES 2

Swapping traditional white rice for brown boosts the nutritional content of this family favourite!
Brown rice has a higher fibre content, which is great for digestion, and has been shown to lower
cholesterol levels and keep our blood-sugar levels stable.

¾ cup brown rice
sea salt
2 teaspoons coconut oil
1 onion, sliced
1 clove garlic, crushed
1 long red chilli, sliced and
  deseeded if you like
1 carrot, peeled and diced
1 small head broccoli, cut into
  small florets, stalks trimmed
½ red capsicum, diced
½ cup fresh or frozen peas
1 tablespoon tamari or soy
  sauce
1 teaspoon sesame oil
  (optional)
2 spring onions, finely chopped
2 × 125 g tins mackerel fillets,
  drained

Place the rice in a saucepan with 1½ cups of water and a pinch of
salt and bring to the boil. Reduce the heat to low, cover and simmer
for 40 minutes. Check that most of the water has been absorbed
and the rice is tender (drain any excess water, or add a bit more and
simmer for another 5 minutes if no excess water).

Meanwhile, heat the coconut oil in a wok over medium heat and
stir-fry the onion for 2–3 minutes, then add the garlic and chilli and
stir-fry for another minute. Add the carrot, broccoli, capsicum and
peas and stir-fry for 4–5 minutes until the veggies are tender but still
have a bit of crunch. Add the rice, tamari or soy sauce and sesame
oil (if using) and stir-fry for 1 minute.

Serve the fried rice topped with the fish and spring onion.

The mackerel fillets can easily be swapped for salmon or tuna.

SMOKED SALMON *and* SESAME SALAD

SERVES 2

This Asian-inspired dish is super-fresh and clean, and the ginger dressing gives it an awesome kick. If you're gluten intolerant, look for 100 per cent buckwheat noodles, as most soba noodles usually contain wheat. You could also substitute the fish for poached chicken. If you bought frozen edamame in Week 1, you should still have some left in your freezer to use here.

⅓ **packet (about 90 g) soba noodles**
1 **Lebanese cucumber, cut into thin ribbons using a vegetable peeler**
1 **handful of snowpeas, trimmed and finely sliced**
½ **cup edamame beans, thawed and podded**
1 **tablespoon sesame seeds**
200 **g smoked salmon**

DRESSING

1 **tablespoon extra virgin olive oil**
¼ **teaspoon sesame oil (optional)**
1 **teaspoon tamari or soy sauce**
1 **teaspoon honey**
1 **teaspoon apple cider vinegar**
2 **teaspoons grated fresh ginger**

To make the dressing, combine all the ingredients in a small bowl and mix well.

Cook the soba noodles in a saucepan of boiling water for 3–4 minutes, then drain and rinse with cool water.

Toss the noodles with the cucumber, snowpeas, edamame and sesame seeds. Pour over the dressing and toss to combine. Top with the smoked salmon and serve.

CHICKEN, CHICKPEA
and ROAST TOMATO SALAD

SERVES 2

This is a wonderfully hearty salad with plenty of protein from the chicken and chickpeas, plus the chickpeas also provide some important fibre. As a bitter green, rocket stimulates enzyme production to improve digestion and help our liver with its natural detoxification process.

1 cup cherry tomatoes
2 teaspoons ground cumin
2 tablespoons extra virgin
  olive oil
sea salt and freshly ground
  black pepper
4 chicken thigh fillets (about
  400 g in total)
1 × 400 g tin chickpeas,
  drained and rinsed
1 carrot, peeled and grated
2 handfuls of rocket
½ avocado, halved

DRESSING
1 tablespoon tahini
1–2 tablespoons hot water
juice of ¼ lemon

Preheat the oven to 200°C and line a baking tray with baking paper.

Place the tomatoes on the prepared tray and bake for 10–15 minutes until collapsing.

Meanwhile, combine the cumin with 1 tablespoon of the olive oil and season with salt and pepper. Rub all over the chicken. Preheat a char-grill pan over medium–high heat and char-grill the chicken for 7–9 minutes on each side until cooked through. Remove from the pan and slice.

To make the dressing, combine all the ingredients in a bowl and mix well.

Combine the chickpeas, carrot and rocket with the remaining olive oil. Place in two bowls and top with the avocado, chicken and roast tomatoes. Drizzle over the tahini dressing to serve.

LAMB CUTLETS *with* TURMERIC COUSCOUS *and* SILVERBEET

SERVES 2

High in iron and B vitamins, lamb cutlets require only a few minutes to cook, making them a quick and easy protein choice. Go for wholegrain couscous if it's available as it is higher in fibre than the regular stuff. A dollop of coconut or Greek yoghurt on the side is a delicious addition.

3 tablespoons ghee or butter
2 sprigs thyme, leaves only
finely grated zest and juice of
  ½ lemon
sea salt and freshly ground
  black pepper
4 lamb cutlets (about 200 g
  in total)
½ cup wholegrain couscous
½ onion, finely diced
1 clove garlic, crushed
1 small green chilli, sliced and
  deseeded if you like
½ teaspoon ground turmeric
4 silverbeet leaves, stalks
  discarded, finely sliced
¼ cup currants
2 tablespoons raw almonds,
  chopped
1 handful of flat-leaf parsley
  leaves
lemon wedges, to serve

Melt 1 tablespoon of the ghee or butter. Combine it with the thyme, lemon zest and juice, and salt and pepper in a small bowl. Lay the lamb chops out on a plate and brush with the mixture, massaging it in with your fingertips. Leave the lamb to marinate in the fridge for 20 minutes to 1 hour (if you have time – this isn't essential).

Place the couscous in a bowl and pour over boiling water to just cover. Place a tea towel over the bowl and leave for 5 minutes, then fluff up the couscous with a fork.

Heat a frying pan over medium heat and add 1 tablespoon of the ghee or butter. Saute the onion for 2 minutes, then add the garlic and chilli and saute for 30 seconds. Add the turmeric and stir well for about 30 seconds, then add the silverbeet leaves. Cook for 2 minutes or until the leaves are starting to wilt. Add the couscous, currants and almonds, then reduce the heat to low and cook for another few minutes, stirring occasionally, while you grill the lamb.

Meanwhile, heat a char-grill pan over medium–high heat and add the remaining ghee or butter. Cook the lamb cutlets for 3 minutes on each side (for medium) or until cooked to your liking.

Stir the parsley through the couscous mixture and serve with the lamb cutlets and some lemon wedges.

MACKEREL *and* CAULIFLOWER COUSCOUS SALAD

SERVES 2

Cauliflower is such a nutritious and versatile vegetable. Not only does it provide us with plenty of fibre, antioxidants and vitamin C, but you can roast it, pan-fry it, stir-fry it or keep it raw and turn it into rice or couscous, as I've done here. Mackerel fillets are a fantastic source of omega-3 fats but you can use any other oily fish you like.

I small cauliflower, cut
  into florets
I carrot, peeled and grated
½ Lebanese cucumber,
  deseeded and diced
¼ red onion, finely diced
2 large handfuls of rocket
I small handful of flat-leaf
  parsley leaves, chopped
I small handful of mint leaves,
  roughly chopped
½ pomegranate, seeds only
3 tablespoons raw pistachio
  kernels, roughly chopped
2 × 125 g tins mackerel fillets,
  drained

DRESSING
1½ tablespoons extra virgin
  olive oil
I tablespoon freshly squeezed
  lemon juice
I teaspoon honey
I clove garlic, crushed
sea salt and freshly ground
  black pepper

To make the dressing, combine all the ingredients in a bowl and mix well

Pulse the cauliflower in a food processor until it resembles couscous – be careful not to turn it into mush.

Place the cauliflower couscous in a large bowl and add the remaining ingredients. Combine well, then stir through the dressing.

Omega-3

Seeds, nuts and fish all provide our bodies with essential omega-3. The Heart Foundation recommends 2–3 serves of fish per week and one plant-based source of omega-3 per day. Our energy level, mood, blood-sugar level, metabolism, insulin level, appetite and immunity can all benefit from a diet high in omega-3, which also helps us produce hormones associated with accelerated fat loss.

CARROT *and* COCONUT SLAW *with* SHREDDED CHICKEN

SERVES 2

Poaching chicken in coconut milk is a fuss-free way to add lots of flavour. If you feel you need a carbohydrate boost after a workout, you can serve this with brown rice. Before shredding up the wombok cabbage, take off 6 of the larger outer leaves and set them aside for tomorrow's lunch of cabbage rolls.

- 1 × 400 g tin organic, full-fat coconut milk
- 2 chicken breasts (about 800 g in total)
- ½ cup desiccated coconut
- ¼ wombok (Chinese) cabbage, shredded
- 1 carrot, peeled and grated
- ½ Lebanese cucumber, sliced into thin batons
- 2 spring onions, finely sliced
- 1 long green chilli, finely sliced and deseeded if you like
- 1 small handful of coriander leaves
- juice of ½ lime

Place the coconut milk in a saucepan over low heat and add the chicken breasts. Add enough water to cover the chicken, then cover with the lid and poach for 10 minutes or until the chicken is cooked through. Remove the chicken, shred it with a fork and leave to cool.

Meanwhile, toast the dessicated coconut in a dry frying pan over low–medium heat for 1–2 minutes until just browned (keep a close eye on this as it can burn quickly). Set aside.

Combine the cabbage, carrot, cucumber, spring onion, chilli, coriander, coconut and shredded chicken in a large bowl. Squeeze over the lime juice and serve.

CREAMY EGG CABBAGE ROLLS

SERVES 2

As a cruciferous vegetable, cabbage is great for the liver and helps the body's detoxification process. These rolls feature a rainbow of coloured vegetables and the creamy egg mixture is unbelievably tasty. If you haven't made the cashew cream use yoghurt or whole egg mayonnaise instead. And feel free to add poached chicken for a little extra protein.

4 organic eggs
2 tablespoons Cashew Cream
  (see page 174)
½ teaspoon dijon mustard
2 tablespoons finely chopped
  flat-leaf parsley
sea salt and freshly ground
  black pepper
6 wombok (Chinese) cabbage
  leaves (see page 222)
2 radishes, trimmed and
  finely sliced
1 carrot, peeled and grated
½ Lebanese cucumber,
  deseeded and grated

Bring a saucepan of water to the boil, then reduce the heat to low. Carefully drop in the eggs and cook for 5–6 minutes (8 minutes if you like them hard-boiled), before cooling under running water. Peel the eggs.

Place the peeled eggs in a bowl with the cashew cream, mustard, parsley and a pinch of salt and pepper. Mash well with a fork.

Remove the tough ends of the cabbage stalks by cutting them out in a V shape.

Fill the top-left third of each wombok leaf with the radish, carrot and cucumber, then add the egg mixture. Roll over once, tuck in the right side, and then keep rolling to enclose the filling.

TUNA *and* MUNG BEAN SALAD

SERVES 2

Warning: this is not your typical (boring) tuna salad recipe! Fibre-rich mung beans bring an interesting crunch to this dish, while the dukkah and currants enliven the taste buds! Brown rice is another awesome source of fibre and provides slow-releasing energy, while tuna ticks off our requirement for protein. Spinach is a good plant-based source of iron – and the parsley is high in vitamin C, so will help us absorb it.

¾ cup brown rice
2 tuna fillets (about 200 g in total) or 2 × 95 g tins tuna in olive oil, drained
½ cup mung beans
2 handfuls of baby spinach
½ avocado, diced
2 tablespoons dukkah
2 tablespoons currants
1 small handful of flat-leaf parsley leaves, finely chopped
1 small handful of mint leaves, finely chopped

DRESSING
1 tablespoon extra virgin olive oil
2 teaspoons balsamic vinegar
1 teaspoon honey
½ teaspoon dijon mustard
sea salt and freshly ground black pepper

To make the dressing, combine all the ingredients in a bowl and mix well.

Place the rice in a saucepan with 1½ cups of water and a pinch of salt, then bring to the boil. Reduce the heat, cover and simmer over low heat for 40 minutes. Check if most of the water has been absorbed and the rice is tender (drain any excess water, or add a bit more and simmer for another 5 minutes if no excess water). Remove from the heat and allow to cool.

Meanwhile, if using fresh tuna, heat a small frying pan over medium–high heat and sear the tuna for 1–2 minutes on each side (longer if you prefer it well done). Remove the tuna from the pan and flake.

If using fresh tuna, combine all the salad ingredients and top with the flaked tuna; if using tinned tuna, combine the brown rice and tuna in a large bowl with the remaining ingredients.

Pour over the dressing to serve.

CITRUS SALAD *with* LENTILS *and* ROCKET

SERVES 2

This fresh and light salad champions the goodness of our citrus fruits. They're high in vitamin C (which helps us absorb the iron from leafy greens) and beta-carotene, an important antioxidant.

2 handfuls of rocket
1 × 400 g tin brown lentils,
   drained and rinsed
¼ red onion, finely sliced
1 small orange, peeled and
   sliced into 1 cm thick rounds
1 small grapefruit, peeled and
   sliced into 1 cm thick rounds
1 small handful of mint leaves,
   finely chopped
3 tablespoons raw pistachio
   kernels, roughly chopped

DRESSING
1 tablespoon extra virgin
   olive oil
1 tablespoon freshly squeezed
   lemon juice
1 teaspoon honey

To make the dressing, combine all the ingredients in a bowl and mix well.

Arrange the rocket over two plates. Scatter the lentils and red onion on top, then add the orange and grapefruit slices. Sprinkle with the mint and pistachios, then drizzle over the dressing.

FIRECRACKER SALAD *with* POACHED CHICKEN

SERVES 4

Poached chicken is an awesome staple to have up your sleeve. It's fast and fuss-free with no oil or grease, and the end result is a lovely tender breast that goes with just about any of your favourite salad combinations! Here we are gathering some serious vitamin firepower from all the vibrant colours in this salad.

POACHED CHICKEN
- 2 × 400 g chicken breasts
- 2.5 cm piece of ginger, peeled
- 2 tablespoons tamari or soy sauce

FIRECRACKER SALAD
- 2 carrots, peeled and cut into thin ribbons using a vegetable peeler
- 1 red capsicum, deseeded and cut into thin matchsticks
- 1 Lebanese cucumber, deseeded and cut into thin matchsticks
- 2 spring onions, finely sliced
- 1 mango, peeled and sliced into thin strips
- 1 cup shredded red cabbage
- 1 cup mung beans
- 4 sprigs mint, leaves picked and torn
- 1 tablespoon black sesame seeds

SWEET CHILLI DRESSING
- 1 tablespoon sweet chilli sauce
- 1 tablespoon tamari or soy sauce
- 2 teaspoons sesame oil
- 3 teaspoons rice wine vinegar

To make the dressing, combine all the ingredients in a bowl and mix well.

Place the chicken breasts in a saucepan with the ginger and tamari or soy sauce and cover with water. Cover with the lid and bring to the boil. Reduce the heat slightly and allow to boil gently for 5 minutes or until cooked through. Remove the pan from the heat and set aside to cool with the lid on while you prepare the salad.

In a bowl, combine the carrot, capsicum, cucumber, spring onion, mango, cabbage and mung beans.

Remove the chicken breasts from the water and shred. Add to the salad and mix well.

Top with the mint and sesame seeds, and drizzle over the dressing to serve.

If you don't feel like carrot ribbons, try spiralising the carrot instead.

QUINOA SUSHI ROLLS

MAKES 2 SUSHI ROLLS

Quinoa is one of my favourite ingredients as it packs an incredible nutritional punch! It's a complete protein, meaning it contains all the amino acids our body needs to do its repair work. Its subtle, nutty flavour goes well with so many foods that if you cook a little too much, it's perfect added to salads or soups the next day. (It's also much quicker to cook than rice!) This is a veggie sushi recipe but you can add any meat or fish you like: poached chicken, fresh salmon and tinned tuna are some of my favourites.

¾ cup quinoa
2 tablespoons rice wine vinegar
1 teaspoon honey
½ avocado
2 teaspoons freshly squeezed
  lime juice
sea salt and freshly ground
  black pepper
2 nori sheets
1 carrot, peeled and cut into
  matchsticks
1 red capsicum, deseeded and
  cut into matchsticks
½ cup alfalfa sprouts
tamari or soy sauce, for dipping
sushi ginger and wasabi,
  to serve (optional)

Rinse the quinoa well and place it in a saucepan with 1½ cups of water. Bring to the boil, then reduce the heat to low and simmer, covered, until the water has been absorbed and the quinoa 'tails' appear, about 12–15 minutes. Remove from the heat and set aside, with the lid on, for 5 minutes. Stir in the rice wine vinegar and honey.

Mash the avocado into a chunky paste with the lime juice, salt and pepper.

To roll the sushi, place a nori sheet on a sushi mat and spread a 1 cm thick layer of quinoa over the mat, leaving 5 mm of space around the borders. Arrange a handful of carrot and capsicum matchsticks, a tablespoon or two of avocado paste and half a handful of alfalfa in a log shape about 3 cm from the bottom edge of the nori sheet. Roll up from the bottom to the top and dab some warm water on the edge of the nori sheet to seal the sushi.

Repeat for the remaining roll, then cut each roll into eight. Serve with soy sauce or tamari for dipping and sushi ginger and wasabi on the side, if you like.

RAINBOW RICE PAPER ROLLS

SERVES 2

This interactive dish is great for when you're having friends and family over for a summery meal!
Perfectly balanced protein, healthy fats and a rainbow of vegetables forms a platter of essential nutrients.

400 g chicken breast
1 tablespoon coconut oil
1 carrot, peeled and cut into matchsticks
1 red or yellow capsicum, deseeded and cut into matchsticks
2 Lebanese cucumbers, deseeded and cut into matchsticks
1 avocado
1 small handful of coriander leaves
1 spring onion, finely chopped
8 rice paper sheets

SWEET CHILLI DIPPING SAUCE

3 tablespoons rice wine vinegar
1 tablespoon tamari or soy sauce
2 tablespoons honey
¼ teaspoon finely minced garlic
1 teaspoon chilli flakes
1 tablespoon water
2 tablespoons freshly squeezed lime juice
pinch of sea salt

To make the dipping sauce, whisk the ingredients together in a small bowl and set aside.

Slice the chicken breast in half to butterfly it, then slice each section through the middle again to create thin sheets.

Heat the coconut oil in a large frying pan over medium–high heat for 1 minute, then add the chicken. Cook for 5 minutes, turning it over after 3 minutes, then remove from the pan and set aside to cool for 10 minutes. When cool, slice into thin strips about 1 cm wide.

Arrange the carrot, capsicum and cucumber matchsticks on a plate. Mash the avocado in a bowl with the coriander and spring onion, and season with salt and pepper.

Fill a wide shallow dish with warm water and lay out a clean damp tea towel next to it.

To assemble your rice paper rolls, take a rice paper sheet and immerse it in the warm water for about 5 seconds. Place the sheet on the tea towel (this prevents it sticking to the bench or table) and arrange the chicken strips, veggie matchsticks and mashed avocado in a small log shape in the bottom third. Holding the filling in place, fold the bottom of the sheet up and start rolling tightly. Around the middle of the sheet, fold the two sides of the sheet on top of the roll then finish rolling to enclose completely.

Dip the rolls into your sweet chilli sauce to enjoy.

It's super-easy to increase your ingredients if you need to feed a crowd!

PUMPKIN, COCONUT and CHILLI SOUP

SERVES 4

This creamy and comforting soup is perfect for a pick-me-up after a hard week of training – or life! Pumpkin is full of fibre, potassium and antioxidants, which promote a healthy immune system; the ginger also helps with this. Chilli only ups the ante, containing vitamins and minerals that aid digestion, fight colds and relieve muscle pain.

1.2 kg butternut pumpkin, peeled and diced into 2–3 cm cubes
1 × 270 g tin organic, full-fat coconut milk
4 cm piece of ginger, peeled and grated
2 long red chillies, finely sliced
2 teaspoons fish sauce
sea salt and freshly ground black pepper
coriander leaves, to serve

Place the pumpkin in a large saucepan and cover with water. Bring to the boil over medium heat, then reduce the heat slightly and simmer for 15 minutes or until softened. Remove from the heat, then drain the pumpkin and mash well. Return to the stovetop over low–medium heat and add the coconut milk, ginger, chilli, fish sauce and 3 cups of water. Season with salt and pepper. Bring to the boil, stirring continuously.

Remove from the heat and carefully transfer to a food processor or high-speed blender, then blitz until you have a smooth and creamy consistency.

Transfer to bowls and top with coriander leaves. Store the extra soup in the fridge for 2–3 days and reheat on the stovetop or in the microwave.

I include most of the red chilli seeds as I love the heat, but if you're sensitive to spice, you might like to leave them out.

MUM'S CHICKEN SOUP *for the* SOUL

SERVES 4

This is my mum's go-to recipe for a nourishing and comforting chicken and vegetable soup. It has a regular spot on my stovetop for its incredible nutritional and feel-good benefits. It uses drumsticks or wings to get all the minerals from the bones, as well as gelatine from the skin, which can help with fatigue, digestion and immunity.

4 chicken drumsticks or
    8–10 chicken wings
2 teaspoons ghee or butter
1 onion, chopped
4 celery stalks, finely sliced
2 potatoes, peeled and diced
2 carrots, peeled and diced
1 cup chopped button
    mushrooms
sea salt and freshly ground
    black pepper
1 × 270 g tin corn kernels
1 litre chicken stock

Wash and pat the chicken pieces dry, then place them in a large saucepan and cover with 1 litre of water. Bring to the boil, then reduce the heat and simmer for 5 minutes or until you see the surface of the water turn slightly foamy. Strain, then remove the chicken from the pan.

Wash the pan and add the ghee or butter. Place over medium heat add the onion and celery and cook for 2–3 minutes until softened. Add the potato, carrot, mushrooms (and any other heavier vegetables you want to add) and cook for another 5 minutes. Season with salt and pepper, then add the corn (and any lighter vegetables), then pour over the chicken stock. Return the chicken to the pan and slowly bring to the boil. Simmer for 5–10 minutes until the vegetables are cooked through.

Divide among bowls to serve, removing the meat from the bones first if you prefer, but I love to leave them in as long as possible to absorb all the minerals they have to offer!

You can use just about any vegetable you have left over in the fridge or freezer! Peas, wombok (Chinese) cabbage, parsnips, pumpkin, leeks, herbs, beans ... the more the merrier!

Dinner

SOY, ORANGE and SESAME SALMON with GREENS and SOBA

SERVES 2

Salmon is a fantastic source of omega-3 fats, as well as being a great protein source. Soba noodles are common in Japanese cuisine; check the ingredients list for 100 per cent buckwheat for a gluten-free choice. For an even lighter option here, omit the noodles and add some extra vegetables. This is a perfectly balanced meal, ticking all the boxes for protein, healthy fats, slow-releasing carbohydrates and veggies!

- 2 tablespoons tamari or soy sauce
- 3 tablespoons freshly squeezed orange juice
- 1 tablespoon honey
- 2 tablespoons sesame seeds
- 1 tablespoon grated fresh ginger
- 1 clove garlic, crushed
- 1 small red chilli, sliced and deseeded if you like
- 2 salmon fillets (about 200 g in total)
- ⅓ packet (90 g) soba noodles
- 2 handfuls of snowpeas, trimmed
- 1 bunch asparagus, trimmed
- 1 bunch bok choy, trimmed
- 2 spring onions, finely chopped

Preheat the oven to 180°C.

Combine the tamari or soy sauce, orange juice, honey, sesame seeds, ginger, garlic and chilli in a small baking dish. Add the salmon fillets and turn to coat in the marinade. Pour the excess marinade into a small saucepan. Place the baking dish in the oven and cook the salmon for 15 minutes or until just cooked through. Heat the remaining marinade over low heat for 3–5 minutes until it thickens (keep an eye on it so it does not burn).

Meanwhile, cook the noodles in a saucepan of boiling water for 3–4 minutes, then drain. Set a steamer over a separate saucepan of simmering water. Place the snowpeas and asparagus in the steamer and steam for 3–4 minutes, then add the bok choy and steam for a further minute.

Serve the salmon fillets with the soba noodles and greens, with the extra marinade spooned over the top and sprinkled with the spring onion.

MARINATED LAMB *with* ROAST BEET SALAD

SAVE LEFTOVERS *for* WED LUNCH

SERVES 4

Lamb backstrap is the busy person's perfect protein! It takes less than 10 minutes to cook and offers an awesome supply of protein, iron, zinc and vitamin B12. Don't skimp on the resting time and you'll be rewarded with super-succulent lamb.

3 tablespoons finely chopped mint
1 tablespoon apple cider vinegar
2 teaspoons honey
2 teaspoons ground cumin
1 teaspoon dijon mustard
sea salt and freshly ground black pepper
2 lamb backstraps (400–500 g in total)
3 beetroots, scrubbed and trimmed
¼ red cabbage, finely shredded
¼ red onion, finely sliced
1 green apple, quartered, cored and finely sliced
4 handfuls of baby spinach
½ cup walnuts

DRESSING

2 tablespoons extra virgin olive oil
1 tablespoon freshly squeezed lemon juice

Preheat the oven to 180°C.

In a bowl, combine the mint, vinegar, honey, cumin and mustard with a pinch of salt and pepper. Add the lamb and coat well, then leave in the fridge to marinate while the beetroot is cooking.

Wrap the beetroot in foil and roast for 40–50 minutes until tender. Remove from the oven, open up the foil and allow to cool while you cook the lamb.

Cook the marinated lamb in a frying pan over medium–high heat for 3–4 minutes each side. Transfer to a plate, cover with foil and rest for 5 minutes.

While the lamb is resting, peel and chop the beetroot and place in a large bowl. Add the cabbage, onion, apple, spinach and walnuts, and combine.

To make the dressing, combine the ingredients in a bowl and mix well.

Slice the lamb, then set half aside, cover and place in the fridge for lunch tomorrow. Drizzle half the dressing over half the salad to serve. Set aside the other half of the dressing and salad to serve with tomorrow's lunch.

Keep the dressing separate so it's still fresh for tomorrow's lunch.

FISH SKEWERS *with* BUCKWHEAT *and* PINEAPPLE SALSA

SERVES 2

A light but flavour-packed dish that's so full of colour! I recommend getting to know your local fishmonger, so you can ask what's fresh and locally caught. They will usually remove the bones for you too. For these skewers, you can use barramundi, snapper, ling, blue eye or orange roughy. Metal or wooden skewers are both fine but if you're using the wooden ones make sure you soak them in water for 30 minutes beforehand to prevent burning.

1 teaspoon smoked paprika
1 teaspoon ground cumin
1 teaspoon dried oregano
1 teaspoon chilli flakes
   (optional)
sea salt and freshly ground
   black pepper
2 firm white fish fillets
   (about 200 g in total),
   cut into 3 cm cubes
½ cup buckwheat groats, rinsed
extra virgin olive oil, for
   drizzling
1 bunch broccolini, trimmed
⅛ pineapple (about 170 g),
   cut into small cubes
½ cup cherry tomatoes,
   quartered
¼ red onion, finely diced
1½ tablespoons finely
   chopped coriander
1½ tablespoons finely
   chopped mint
½ long green chilli, sliced
   and deseeded if you like
juice of 1 lime

On a plate, combine the paprika, cumin, oregano and chilli flakes (if using) with a pinch of salt and pepper. Toss the fish in the spices and leave in the fridge while you prepare the buckwheat.

Place the buckwheat in a small saucepan with 1 cup of water. Bring to the boil, then reduce the heat to low and simmer over low heat for about 10 minutes or until the water has been absorbed. Remove from the heat and set aside, uncovered, for 5 minutes, then fluff with a fork.

Remove the fish from the fridge, thread onto the skewers and drizzle with olive oil. Heat a frying pan or char-grill pan over medium–high heat. Drizzle the broccolini with oil and pan-fry for 2 minutes on each side, then add the fish skewers and cook, turning them, for 4 minutes each side (keep turning the broccolini too) or until cooked through.

Combine the buckwheat with the pineapple, tomatoes, onion, coriander, mint, chilli and half the lime juice. Arrange on a plate and top with the broccolini and fish skewers. Squeeze over the remaining lime juice just before serving.

If you don't have skewers on hand, you can just pan-fry the fish fillets.

OREGANO *and* LEMON CHICKEN *with* GRILLED VEGGIES

SAVE
LEFTOVERS
for FRI
LUNCH

SERVES 4

This recipe proves you don't have to be a chef to make really tasty food! It's so easy to prepare and the grilled flavours make a nice change from steamed veg – the slightly smoky taste never disappoints me! To make dinner even easier, prepare your marinade in the morning and leave it in the fridge. This serves 4, so keep half aside for lunch tomorrow.

8 chicken thigh fillets (about 800 g in total)
2 tablespoons dried oregano
finely grated zest and juice of 1 lemon
2 cloves garlic, crushed
1 tablespoon extra virgin olive oil
sea salt and freshly ground black pepper
1 eggplant, sliced into 1 cm rounds
1 red capsicum, deseeded and thickly sliced
1 yellow capsicum, deseeded and thickly sliced
1 large zucchini, sliced lengthways into 5 mm thick strips
550 g butternut pumpkin, cut into 5 mm thick slices
1 tablespoon extra virgin olive oil (if char-grilling), plus extra for drizzling
lemon wedges, to serve

Place the chicken in a bowl and add the oregano, lemon zest, garlic, olive oil and a pinch of salt and pepper. Leave in the fridge to marinate for at least 20 minutes.

Using a barbecue or a large char-grill pan, grill the veggies in batches for about 3–4 minutes each side until charred and cooked through. If you're using a barbecue, add the chicken and cook for 3–4 minutes each side until cooked through; if using a char-grill pan, remove the veggies and keep them warm in the oven at 100°C, then add the olive oil and char-grill the chicken for 3–4 minutes on each side until cooked through.

Set half aside for lunch tomorrow, and plate up the rest on a platter with a drizzle of olive oil and some lemon wedges.

BEEF *with* CAULIFLOWER PUREE, HAZELNUTS *and* POMEGRANATE

SERVES 2

I love the silky smooth texture of cauliflower puree, and it's a superb way to incorporate more veg into your diet. Here it works perfectly with the crunchy hazelnuts and juicy pomegranate seeds. To extract the pomegranate seeds, cut the pomegranate horizontally with the stalk at the top. Hold it, cut-side down, over a bowl in the sink and bash the outside shell with a heavy spoon or rolling pin – then just watch the seeds fall into the bowl underneath.

3 tablespoons hazelnuts
½ cauliflower, florets roughly cut into chunks
200 g lean rump steak
2 teaspoons ground cumin
1 tablespoon extra virgin olive oil
1 handful of green beans, trimmed
1 bunch asparagus, trimmed
3 tablespoons almond milk or milk of your choice
sea salt and freshly ground black pepper
½ pomegranate, seeds only
1 handful of flat-leaf parsley leaves

Preheat the oven to 180°C.

Lay the hazelnuts on a baking tray and toast for 10 minutes or until lightly coloured. Wrap in a clean tea towel and leave for 1 minute. Rub the nuts in the tea towel to remove any loose skins and set aside to cool, then chop.

Set a steamer over a saucepan of simmering water. Place the cauliflower in the steamer and steam until very tender, about 15 minutes.

Meanwhile, sprinkle the beef with the cumin and drizzle with the olive oil. Preheat a char-grill or frying pan over medium–high heat and cook the beef for 3 minutes on each side or until cooked to your liking, then remove from the pan and rest for 3 minutes before slicing.

Transfer the cauliflower to a food processor or high-speed blender, then place the beans and asparagus in the steamer and steam for 2–3 minutes until tender. Add the almond milk and a good pinch of salt and pepper to the cauliflower and blitz until smooth.

Serve the beef with the beans, asparagus and cauliflower puree, with the hazelnuts, pomegranate seeds and parsley sprinkled over.

THAI CHICKEN LETTUCE CUPS

SERVES 2

Where possible I recommend leaner breast meat rather than thigh for your chicken mince – just ask your butcher. If miso is a new ingredient for you, then welcome to the world of fermented goodness! Fermented products like miso help to keep up the healthy bacteria in our gut, which allows us to maximise digestion of all the nutrients in our food.

¼ packet (about 30 g) vermicelli noodles, broken into 2–3 cm lengths
1 teaspoon coconut oil
1 tablespoon grated fresh ginger
1 small lemongrass stalk, white part finely chopped
1 long red chilli, finely chopped and deseeded if you like, plus extra for garnish (optional)
1 clove garlic, finely chopped
200 g chicken mince
½ carrot, peeled and grated
1 red capsicum, deseeded and diced
2 spring onions, chopped
1 handful of coriander leaves, chopped, plus extra for garnish
1 handful of mint leaves, chopped, plus extra for garnish
juice of ½ lime
2 teaspoons tamari or soy sauce
2 teaspoons fish sauce
1 teaspoon honey
½ iceberg lettuce, separated into cups
chopped unsalted peanuts or raw cashews, to serve (optional)

SAUCE
2 teaspoons miso paste (light/shiro)
1½ tablespoons almond butter
½ teaspoon mirin
½ teaspoon apple cider vinegar
1–2 tablespoons hot water

To make the sauce, place all the ingredients in a bowl and stir well until combined, adding more water, a teaspoon at a time, if needed.

Fill a bowl with boiling water and soak the noodles for 5–10 minutes or until soft, then drain.

Meanwhile, heat a frying pan over medium heat and add the coconut oil. Add the ginger, lemongrass, chilli and garlic and fry for 1–2 minutes. Add the chicken mince, breaking up any lumps and cook for 2–3 minutes until just browned, then add the carrot, capsicum, spring onion, herbs, lime juice, tamari or soy sauce, fish sauce and honey. Add the vermicelli noodles and cook for another 1–2 minutes.

Fill each lettuce cup with the chicken noodle mixture and top with the sauce, extra herbs, nuts and extra chilli, if using.

Don't waste the rest of your lemongrass stalks - add them with a slice of ginger to your next herbal tea!

PESTO PRAWN PASTA

SERVES 2

Prawns are not only a great source of protein but they are high in selenium, which promotes muscle metabolism and heart health – plus they are so quick to prepare. Ensure you look for Australian prawns rather than imported as the fishing methods are more strictly regulated in Australia than other countries. We've got the best of both worlds with a mix of wholegrain pasta and zucchini noodles here, but feel free to vary the ratio to find the right balance for you. The chilli pesto delivers the perfect hit of spice to take this simple dish to the next level.

250 g wholegrain pasta
1 large zucchini, sliced into spaghetti or spiralised (see note below)
1 tablespoon extra virgin olive oil
1 clove garlic, crushed
200 g green (raw) prawns, shelled and deveined
3 tablespoons Kale and Almond Chilli Pesto (see page 194)
2 handfuls of rocket

Bring a saucepan of water to the boil and cook the pasta according to the packet instructions. In the final couple of minutes, add the zucchini. Drain, reserving 3 tablespoons of the cooking liquid.

Return the pan to medium heat and add the olive oil and garlic. Cook for 1 minute, then add the prawns and cook for 2–3 minutes until they are pink. Finally add the pasta, zucchini, pesto, cooking liquid and rocket. Mix well and serve.

Make sure you look for prawns that have not been imported.

No spiraliser? No stress!

If you don't have a spiraliser, there's no reason to miss out on the zucchini noodle action! Simply grab your vegetable peeler and, holding the top of the zucchini, run lengthways to peel long ribbons of zucchini. You can serve as is, or lay your ribbons flat and carefully slice lengthways to create noodles.

SATAY TOFU RICE PAPER ROLLS

SERVES 2

Fresh and crunchy rice paper rolls are the perfect dinner for a hot summer night. Once you get the knack of rolling them, they're super-easy! The trick is to place your ingredients horizontally across the paper about 4 cm from the top, roll the top over once, fold in the sides and then keep rollin'! Tofu is a great plant-based protein, but you can always substitute chicken, prawns or beef.

1 tablespoon tamari or
soy sauce
250 g firm tofu, cut into
2 cm fingers
1 tablespoon coconut oil
½ small wombok (Chinese)
cabbage, shredded
1 carrot, peeled and cut into
thin matchsticks
½ red capsicum, finely sliced
2 spring onions, finely chopped
1 handful of Thai basil leaves
(optional)
1 handful of coriander leaves
1 lime, halved
8 rice paper rounds

SATAY SAUCE
½ teaspoon coconut oil
¼ red onion, diced
1 clove garlic, crushed
1 teaspoon grated fresh ginger
1 small red chilli, diced
1 teaspoon grated fresh
turmeric or ½ teaspoon
ground turmeric
3 tablespoons almond butter
¾ cup coconut milk
1 teaspoon rice wine vinegar
1 teaspoon tamari or soy sauce
1 tablespoon maple syrup

Pour the tamari or soy sauce over the tofu and leave it in the fridge for 1 hour (or at least 5 minutes).

To make the satay sauce, heat the coconut oil in a small saucepan over low–medium heat. Add the onion and fry for 2–3 minutes, then add the garlic, ginger, chilli and turmeric and fry for 1 minute. Remove from the heat and stir in the almond butter. Add the coconut milk, vinegar, tamari or soy sauce and maple syrup, then place over low heat and stir frequently until the sauce thickens slightly.

Heat the coconut oil in a frying pan over medium–high heat, add the tofu and fry for 2–3 minutes on each side until browned.

Lay the vegetables out on a platter with the tofu, herbs, lime and satay sauce. Serve on the table with the rice paper and a bowl of hot water. Soften a sheet of paper in hot water and then get rolling – layering vegetables, tofu, sauce, herbs and a squeeze of lime.

CHICKEN PAD THAI

SERVES 4

This is the perfect way to enjoy a pad thai with the confidence that you've made it yourself without any nasty ingredients. I love packing in extra veggies for a nutritional boost.

150 g rice stick noodles
2 tablespoons tamari or
    soy sauce
I teaspoon fish sauce
2 teaspoons coconut sugar
I lime, ½ juiced, ½ cut into
    4 wedges
I tablespoon coconut oil
400 g chicken thigh fillets,
    cut into 2 cm pieces
I long red chilli, finely sliced
2 cloves garlic, finely sliced
I red onion, sliced into thin
    wedges
I carrot, peeled and cut into
    thin matchsticks
2 handfuls of snowpeas,
    trimmed and cut into
    thin strips
2 organic eggs, lightly beaten
2 handfuls of bean sprouts
3 tablespoons roughly chopped
    raw cashews

Soak the noodles in boiling water for 5 minutes, then drain and set aside.

Combine the tamari or soy sauce, fish sauce, coconut sugar and lime juice and set aside.

Heat the coconut oil in a wok over high heat. Cook the chicken for 3–4 minutes until browned on all sides, then remove from the wok.

Reduce the heat to medium and add the chilli, garlic and onion to the wok. Stir-fry for 1 minute, then add the carrot and snowpeas and stir-fry for a further 2–3 minutes. Add the noodles and the sauce and mix well. Add the chicken, then slowly pour in the eggs and stir-fry for 1 minute. Lastly, add the bean sprouts.

Set half aside for lunch tomorrow, and plate up with the cashews and lime wedges to serve.

PORK FILLET *with* GARLIC MUSHROOMS *and* APPLE SLAW

SERVES 2

Mushrooms are beneficial to our immune system as they can help eliminate toxins from the body, plus they provide us with vitamin D. They are deliciously tender when roasted. Rosemary and garlic are the perfect flavour pairing.

4 field mushrooms, stems
    removed
2 tablespoons extra virgin
    olive oil
1 sprig rosemary, leaves
    chopped
2 cloves garlic, sliced
2 × 300 g pork fillets, cut in half
½ small wombok (Chinese)
    cabbage, shredded
4 kale leaves, stalks discarded,
    shredded
1 green apple, cored and grated
¼ red onion, finely sliced
2 radishes, trimmed and
    finely sliced
1 handful of flat-leaf parsley
    leaves
1 handful of mint leaves

DRESSING

1½ tablespoons extra virgin
    olive oil
2 teaspoons apple cider vinegar
juice of ½ lemon
1 teaspoon honey
sea salt and freshly ground
    black pepper

Preheat the oven to 180°C.

Place the mushrooms on a baking tray, drizzle with 1 tablespoon of the olive oil and scatter over the rosemary and garlic.

Heat the remaining olive oil in a frying pan over medium–high heat and sear the pork for 2 minutes, turning until browned all over. Place on the baking tray with the mushrooms.

Roast in the oven for 10 minutes or until the pork is cooked through, then remove and rest the pork for 3 minutes. Remove the mushrooms from the oven once the pork is ready.

To make the dressing, combine all the ingredients in a bowl and mix well.

Combine the cabbage, kale, apple, onion, radish, parsley and mint, then pour over the dressing. Serve the slaw with the pork and mushrooms.

BEEF *and* EGGPLANT LASAGNE

SERVES 4

The deep-purple skins of eggplant provide an awesome hit of antioxidants, and this delicious nightshade vegetable is also a great source of fibre. Here we slice the eggplant to resemble sheets of pasta and layer it with a rich tomato sauce for the perfect veggie-packed lasagne, all topped with a cauliflower bechamel sauce. If you like dairy, feel free to sprinkle a small handful of cheese over the top to get some browning action! Keep half of this for lunch tomorrow.

3 eggplants, sliced into thin rounds
3 tablespoons extra virgin olive oil
1 onion, finely diced
2 cloves garlic, crushed
1 sprig rosemary, leaves finely chopped
500 g beef mince
1½ × 400 g tins diced tomatoes
½ × 140 g jar tomato paste
1 red capsicum, deseeded and finely diced
1 handful of basil leaves
1 bay leaf (optional)
2 cups baby spinach
1 cauliflower, cut into florets
2 tablespoons milk of your choice, plus extra if needed
pinch of ground nutmeg
sea salt and freshly ground black pepper

Preheat the oven to 180°C.

Lay the eggplant slices on two large baking trays then drizzle with 2 tablespoons of the olive oil and bake for 15 minutes, turning halfway, then remove from the oven.

Meanwhile, prepare the sauce. Add the remaining olive oil to a large frying pan over medium–high heat, add the onion, garlic and rosemary, and saute for 5 minutes or until soft. Add the beef mince, breaking it up with a wooden spoon, and cook until just browned, about 2–3 minutes. Add the tinned tomatoes, tomato paste, capsicum, basil and bay leaf, if using (you can also add up to ½ cup of water if the sauce seems too thick). Leave to simmer over low heat for 15–20 minutes until the lasagne is ready to be assembled, adding the spinach in the final couple of minutes, and discarding the bay leaf.

While the sauce is simmering, set a steamer over a saucepan of simmering water. Place the cauliflower in the steamer and steam until very tender, about 15 minutes. Transfer the cauliflower to a food processor and add the milk, nutmeg and a good pinch of salt and pepper. Blitz until smooth, then set aside (you may need to add a touch more milk for a smoother consistency).

To assemble the lasagne, take a 20 cm × 30 cm baking dish and line the base with a quarter of the eggplant rounds. Pour in a third of the sauce and then layer twice more with eggplant and sauce, and a final layer of eggplant. Pour the cauliflower mixture on top and smooth out with a spoon. Bake in the oven for 20 minutes or until bubbling at the sides.

Remember to save the leftover ½ tin of diced tomatoes (put them in an airtight container in the fridge) and the leftover ½ jar of tomato paste for Sunday night.

PRAWN *and* BROCCOLI STIR-FRY

SERVES 2

Stir-fries are an epic one-pot dinner and a genius way to use leftover veg and pack lots of different colours into your meals. I love to ramp up the spice, but if you're not a fan simply omit the seeds from the chilli. Another secret weapon in this dish is ginger, a natural antibiotic that helps to reduce toxins and promote circulation and immunity.

2 teaspoons coconut oil
200 g green (raw) prawns, shelled and deveined
1 long red chilli, sliced
2 cm piece of ginger, peeled and grated
2 cloves garlic, finely sliced
1 small head broccoli, cut into florets, stalks trimmed
⅛ red cabbage, shredded
1 carrot, peeled and cut into matchsticks
4 spring onions, sliced
⅓ packet (about 90 g) soba noodles
1 small handful of Thai basil leaves (optional), plus extra to serve
1 handful of coriander leaves, plus extra to serve
2 tablespoons tamari or soy sauce
2 teaspoons coconut sugar
2 tablespoons sesame seeds

Bring a small saucepan of water to the boil.

Heat a wok over medium heat, add the coconut oil and stir-fry the prawns, chilli, ginger and garlic for 2–3 minutes until the prawns change colour. Remove from the wok. Add the broccoli, cabbage, carrot and spring onion and toss until the vegetables are just tender but still with a bit of crunch, about 3–4 minutes.

Meanwhile, cook the soba noodles in the saucepan of boiling water for 4 minutes, then drain and rinse. Add the basil (if using), coriander, tamari or soy sauce, coconut sugar, sesame seeds, prawns and soba noodles to the wok and toss to combine.

Serve with extra basil and coriander.

BAKED OCEAN TROUT
with VEGGIES *and* KALE CHIPS

SERVES 2

Ocean trout is another awesome oily fish that provides us with those essential omega-3 fatty acids, but you can substitute any other kind of fish here, no worries. To speed up cooking time, prep your fish parcel in advance and leave it in the fridge until you're ready to pop it in the oven. Kale chips are a super-easy healthy snack to have on hand – feel free to make extra here to use as snacks!

1 bunch thin asparagus, trimmed (or smaller bunch thick asparagus, trimmed and halved lengthways)

1 zucchini, cut into thin ribbons using a vegetable peeler

2 tablespoons extra virgin olive oil

2 ocean trout fillets (about 200 g in total)

1 lemon, sliced

1 handful of cherry tomatoes

3 tablespoons pitted black olives

sea salt and freshly ground black pepper

4 kale leaves, stalks discarded, torn

1 handful of basil leaves

Cut out two 30 cm × 30 cm squares of baking paper and foil. Place one baking paper square on top of each piece of foil. Place the asparagus on top of each square, then the zucchini. Lay the fish on top, drizzle with 1 tablespoon of the olive oil and then place the lemon slices over the fish. Scatter over the tomatoes and olives, and add a pinch of salt and pepper. Fold up the foil and baking paper to fully enclose.

When ready to cook, preheat the oven to 180°C.

Bake the fish in the oven for 15–20 minutes until cooked to your liking.

Meanwhile, toss the kale leaves in the remaining olive oil and season with salt and pepper. Spread out on a baking tray and bake for 5–10 minutes until just browning and crispy (watch carefully as they can burn quickly!).

Serve the fish in the baking paper topped with kale chips and basil.

BLACK BEAN *and* SWEET POTATO NACHOS

SERVES 2

Bring a festive Mexican feel to your Sunday dinner with this healthy take on nachos. Black beans are a great source of vegetarian protein and are also very high in fibre. For super-crispy sweet potato chips, try and hunt down a purple sweet potato if you can, but the orange is just as delicious and nutritious!

1 purple sweet potato, peeled and cut into wedges
2 tablespoons extra virgin olive oil
1 small onion, diced
2 cloves garlic, crushed
½ jalapeno chilli, finely chopped
2 teaspoons smoked paprika
1 teaspoon ground coriander
1 teaspoon ground cumin
1 × 400 g tin black beans, drained and rinsed
1 small red capsicum, deseeded and diced
½ × 400 g tin diced tomatoes
½ × 140 g jar tomato paste
½ avocado
sea salt and freshly ground black pepper
juice of ½ lime
1 handful of coriander leaves
lime wedges, to serve

Preheat the oven to 180°C.

Spread the sweet potato wedges on a baking tray and drizzle with 1 tablespoon of the olive oil. Bake for 40–45 minutes until browned and tender.

Meanwhile, heat a frying pan over medium heat, add the remaining olive oil and fry the onion for 2 minutes. Add the garlic and chilli and continue to cook for 1 minute. Add the paprika, ground coriander and cumin and stir through for 30 seconds, then add the black beans, capsicum, diced tomatoes and tomato paste and stir well. Reduce the heat to low and stir until the vegetables are cooked and the beans are heated through.

While the bean mixture is cooking, prepare the avocado by mashing it with some salt and pepper and the lime juice.

Spoon the bean mixture into bowls and top with the avocado and coriander. Serve with a wedge of lime and use the sweet potato chips to dip in!

Remember to use the diced tomatoes and tomato paste left over from Thursday night.

BARRAMUNDI *with* ROAST PUMPKIN, ASPARAGUS *and* POMEGRANATE

SERVES 2

Barramundi is a wild-caught fish, which makes it a very sustainable seafood option. Here its crispy skin paired with the softness of the roasted pumpkin is a great combo. The bioflavonoid in asparagus strengthens our immune system and the pomegranate provides an incredible burst of flavour as well as vitamins A, C and E.

½ small kent (jap) pumpkin, cut into 4 thick wedges
1 tablespoon extra virgin olive oil
sea salt and freshly ground black pepper
1 bunch asparagus, trimmed
2 teaspoons butter or ghee
2 barramundi fillets (about 200 g in total)
½ pomegranate, seeds only
mint leaves, to serve

BALSAMIC GLAZE
2 tablespoons freshly squeezed orange juice
2 tablespoons maple syrup
1 tablespoon balsamic vinegar

Preheat the oven to 180°C.

Place the pumpkin wedges on a baking tray, drizzle with the olive oil and sprinkle with salt and pepper. Roast for 30–40 minutes until tender, adding the asparagus to the tray in the final 10 minutes (15 minutes if they are thick spears).

Meanwhile, to make the balsamic glaze, place all the ingredients in a saucepan and bring to the boil over medium heat. Reduce the heat to low and simmer for 5 minutes or until thickened, then set aside.

Heat the butter or ghee in a frying pan over medium heat and cook the fish, skin-side down, for 2–3 minutes then turn and cook for a further 2–3 minutes, until cooked to your liking. Remove the pan from the heat and leave the fish to rest for 1 minute.

Plate up the pumpkin wedges and asparagus, then the fish, drizzle over the balsamic glaze and finish with the pomegranate seeds and mint leaves.

This balsamic glaze is also delicious drizzled over smashed avo on toast!

LAMB KOFTAS *with* CAULIFLOWER PILAF

SERVES 2

Pilaf is a Turkish dish traditionally cooked with rice, but I've swapped it with cauliflower to boost our vegetable intake. I love incorporating different spices into my cooking, and turmeric is one with serious skills! It's got anti-inflammatory, anti-ageing properties and, along with cauliflower, is calming for our digestive systems.

250 g lamb mince
1 small carrot, peeled
and grated
½ onion, finely diced
½ long red chilli, finely diced
1 teaspoon ground cumin
1 teaspoon ground coriander
1 small handful of mint leaves,
finely chopped
1 tablespoon ghee or butter
lemon wedges, to serve

YOGHURT SAUCE
3 tablespoons coconut yoghurt
(or full-fat unsweetened
Greek yoghurt)
finely grated zest of ½ lemon
1 teaspoon honey
1 spring onion, finely sliced
pinch of sea salt

CAULIFLOWER PILAF
1 small cauliflower, cut into
florets
1 tablespoon ghee or butter
2 teaspoons brown mustard
seeds
2 teaspoons grated fresh ginger
1 clove garlic, crushed
1 teaspoon chilli flakes
½ teaspoon ground turmeric
1 small handful of fresh curry
leaves, lightly crushed
juice of ½ lemon

To make the yoghurt sauce, combine all the ingredients in a small bowl and set aside.

To make the cauliflower pilaf, pulse the cauliflower in a food processor until it resembles rice (be careful not to blitz it too finely or it will become mushy).

In a bowl, combine the mince, carrot, onion, chilli, cumin, coriander and mint. Shape heaped tablespoons of the mixture into small koftas. Heat the ghee or butter in a frying pan over medium heat and cook the koftas for about 8 minutes, turning to cook evenly.

Meanwhile, continue with the cauliflower pilaf. Heat the ghee or butter in a large frying pan over medium heat. Add the mustard seeds and fry until they begin to pop, then stir in the ginger, garlic and chilli flakes and fry for 1–2 minutes. Add the turmeric and curry leaves and fry for another 1–2 minutes, then add the cauliflower rice, lemon juice and 2½ tablespoons of water. Stir to combine and cook, stirring occasionally, for 5 minutes.

Serve the koftas with the cauliflower pilaf and yoghurt sauce, with lemon wedges for squeezing.

CHICKEN and GRAPE SALAD

SAVE LEFTOVERS for THURS LUNCH

SERVES 4

Adding fruit like grapes and pomegranate seeds to salads is a clever way to bring some natural sweetness and juice to the dish, without the need for artificial sauces or dressings. The leafy greens here are alkalising and nourishing for our digestive systems, and couscous is a nice change from quinoa and buckwheat to keep your taste buds feeling inspired. Keep the dressing on the side so that the salad stays fresh for tomorrow's lunch.

I cup wholegrain couscous
I tablespoon dried oregano
finely grated zest of I lemon
I tablespoon extra virgin
   olive oil
2 chicken breasts (about
   800 g in total), halved
   lengthways through the
   middle
2 handfuls of green grapes,
   halved
4 handfuls of mixed lettuce
2 celery stalks, finely sliced
I avocado, sliced
½ pomegranate, seeds only

DRESSING

2 tablespoons extra virgin
   olive oil
I tablespoon balsamic vinegar
I teaspoon honey
I teaspoon dijon mustard
sea salt and freshly ground
   black pepper

To make the dressing, combine all the ingredients in a bowl and mix well.

Boil the kettle and place the couscous in a small heatproof bowl. Pour just enough boiled water over the couscous to cover. Cover the bowl with a clean tea towel and leave for 5 minutes, then fluff the couscous with a fork.

Meanwhile, combine the oregano and lemon zest with the olive oil and rub into the chicken. Preheat a char-grill pan over medium heat and cook the chicken for 4–5 minutes on each side until cooked through. Remove from the heat and slice.

Combine the grapes, lettuce, celery, avocado, pomegranate seeds and couscous. Set aside half the salad and chicken for tomorrow's lunch.

Pour the dressing over the salad when ready to serve and top with the chicken.

BAKED LEMON FISH *with* SWEET POTATO MASH *and* MIXED PEAS

SERVES 2

Oven-baking fish in a bag is a fantastic way to lock in flavours and moisture without the need for any oils. Fish is one of my favourite sources of protein, which is essential for growth and repair and maintaining healthy muscles. The iodine content in fish supports thyroid function. Ask your fishmonger for a sustainably caught fish that works well for baking.

2 tablespoons extra virgin olive oil

2 lemons, 1 juiced, 1 sliced

4 sprigs thyme, leaves picked and chopped

1 clove garlic, crushed

sea salt and freshly ground black pepper

2 firm white fish fillets (about 200 g in total)

1 small sweet potato, peeled and cut into small chunks

1 cup peas

2 handfuls of sugar snap peas

1 handful of mint leaves

Preheat the oven to 200°C.

Whisk 1 tablespoon of the olive oil with the lemon juice, thyme, garlic and some salt and pepper. Cut two 30 cm squares each of foil and baking paper. Lay a square of baking paper on top of each square of foil. Place the fish in the middle of each, pour over the lemon dressing and add the lemon slices. Enclose to make two parcels. Bake the fish for 12–15 minutes until it starts to flake.

Meanwhile, set a steamer over a saucepan of simmering water. Place the sweet potato in the steamer and steam until very tender, about 10 minutes. Remove from the steamer (but keep the water simmering) and transfer to a bowl or saucepan, then mash with a drizzle of olive oil and some salt and pepper.

When the fish is almost ready, add the peas and sugar snap peas to the steamer and steam for 1–2 minutes. Toss with the remaining olive oil.

Serve the baked fish with the sweet potato mash and mixed peas topped with fresh mint.

DUKKAH-CRUSTED STEAK *with* BEET CHIPS *and* GREEN BEANS

SERVES 2

Dukkah – a traditional Egyptian mix of spices, nuts and seeds – gives these steaks a delicious crust. Beetroot is a fantastic anti-inflammatory that helps with cleansing the blood and liver function. The beet chips make the most beautiful side dish! If you're not keen on haloumi, you can use goat's cheese instead.

2 beetroots, scrubbed, trimmed, and very finely sliced into rounds

1 tablespoon extra virgin olive oil

sea salt and freshly ground black pepper

2 eye fillet steaks (about 200 g in total)

3 tablespoons dukkah

2 teaspoons ghee or butter

2 handfuls of green beans, trimmed

100 g haloumi, sliced into four slices (optional)

Preheat the oven to 180°C.

Lay the beetroot discs out in a single layer on two large baking trays, drizzle with the olive oil and season with salt and pepper. Bake for 25 minutes, turning once, or until slightly browned and crispy.

Coat the steaks evenly in the dukkah. Heat an ovenproof chargrill pan over medium–high heat. Add 1 teaspoon of the ghee or butter and cook the dukkah-crusted steak for 2–3 minutes on each side. Transfer the pan to the oven and cook for 5 minutes, for medium–rare (or until cooked to your liking; cooking times may vary depending on the thickness of your steak). Transfer to a plate and cover with foil to rest for 5 minutes.

Place the pan back over the heat and add the remaining ghee or butter. Cook the beans for 5–6 minutes or until slightly charred and tender. In the final couple of minutes, add the haloumi, if using, and cook for 1 minute on each side or until charred.

Serve the steak with the green beans, haloumi and beetroot chips on the side.

TURKEY MEATBALL GREEN CURRY

SERVES 2

I love the warming comfort of a homemade curry and when I have time I like to make my curry paste from scratch. But we're all busy so, if you need to, look for a premade jar variety that has only ingredients you recognise. If you do make the paste from scratch it will last for 4–5 days in the fridge. Bean sprouts are often packaged in large quantities but don't last very long, so try and hunt out a small packet or visit a greengrocer where you can serve yourself. Serve this with brown rice if you feel like an extra carbohydrate fix after a workout.

250 g turkey mince
1 handful of coriander leaves, finely chopped
2 spring onions, finely diced
1 clove garlic, crushed
1 tablespoon coconut oil
3 tablespoons green curry paste (see recipe below or use good-quality shop-bought)
200 ml organic, full-fat coconut milk
2 teaspoons fish sauce
juice of ½ lime, plus lime wedges, to serve
½ red capsicum, cut into 2 cm chunks
1 handful of snowpeas, trimmed
2–3 silverbeet leaves, stalks discarded, sliced
1 handful of basil leaves, roughly chopped
1 handful of bean sprouts

GREEN CURRY PASTE
1 lemongrass stalk, white part chopped
1 tablespoon chopped fresh ginger
2 long green chillies, chopped
2 kaffir lime leaves, spine removed, chopped
1 red shallot, diced
1 teaspoon ground cumin
2 cloves garlic, crushed
½ bunch coriander, stems and roots scraped clean

To make the green curry paste, blitz all the ingredients and 2 tablespoons of water in a food processor or pound using a mortar and pestle until it forms a paste. This makes about ½ cup.

Combine the turkey mince, coriander, spring onion and garlic in a bowl. Mix well, then roll into 3 cm meatballs.

Heat the coconut oil in a wok over medium–high heat. Add 3 tablespoons curry paste and cook for 30 seconds, then increase the heat and add the meatballs. Stir-fry for 6–7 minutes, until they are just browned all over.

Reduce the heat to low and add the coconut milk, fish sauce and lime juice (if your coconut milk is a thick one you may need to add 3 tablespoons of water here too). Cook for another 2 minutes or until the meatballs are cooked through.

Add the capsicum, snowpeas, silverbeet and basil and stir for another 3 minutes or until the veggies are just tender.

Serve with the bean sprouts and lime wedges.

SALMON NICOISE PLATTER

SERVES 2

A Nicoise salad has the perfect balance of macronutrients: protein from the eggs and salmon, carbohydrates from the potato, healthy fats from the olives and the dressing, plus a rainbow of different vegetables. It also features cooked and raw foods, which are both important in a balanced diet. This also makes a great picnic platter – why not take it down to the park or beach and watch the sun set?

6 chat potatoes, halved
1 handful of green beans, trimmed
1 bunch asparagus, trimmed
2 organic eggs,
2 teaspoons ghee or butter
2 skinless salmon fillets (about 200 g in total)
100 g haloumi, cut into four slices (optional)
3 tablespoons pitted black olives
¼ red onion, finely sliced
½ cup cherry tomatoes
6 cos lettuce leaves
1 handful of flat-leaf parsley leaves

DRESSING

1½ tablespoons extra virgin olive oil
2 teaspoons apple cider vinegar
1 heaped teaspoon dijon mustard
sea salt and freshly ground black pepper

To make the dressing, combine all the ingredients in a bowl and mix well.

Set a steamer over a saucepan of simmering water. Place the potatoes in the steamer and steam for 15 minutes, then add the beans and asparagus to the steamer and steam for a further 5 minutes until all the veggies are just tender.

Meanwhile, bring a saucepan of water to the boil, then reduce the heat to low. Carefully drop in the eggs and cook for 7–8 minutes. Rinse under cold water, then peel the eggs and slice them in half lengthways.

Heat the ghee or butter in a frying pan over medium–high heat and add the salmon. Cook for 4–5 minutes, then turn and cook for another 4–5 minutes for medium, or until cooked to your liking. In the final minute, add the haloumi, if using, and cook on both sides. Remove from the pan and flake the salmon into pieces.

Arrange the veggies, eggs, salmon, haloumi, olives, onion, tomatoes, lettuce and parsley on a platter and drizzle the dressing over.

FALAFELS *with* GREEN SAUCE *in* LETTUCE CUPS

SAVE
LEFTOVERS
for TUE
LUNCH

SERVES 4

Restaurant falafels are often deep-fried and served with lots of pita bread and heavy sauces. This dish is all about taking the delicious flavours and removing those ingredients that have no real nutritional value. Pan-frying the falafels and serving them in lettuce cups keeps them light and this green sauce is packed with healthy fats. Keep the leftovers in the fridge for tomorrow's lunch: reheat in the oven at 160°C for 10–15 minutes and serve with lettuce cups.

2 × 400 g tins chickpeas,
  drained and rinsed
2 cloves garlic, crushed
1 long red chilli, finely chopped
  and deseeded if you like
2 teaspoons ground cumin
1 teaspoon ground turmeric
½ teaspoon paprika
1 small handful of coriander
  leaves, plus extra to serve
1 small handful of mint leaves
½ cup sourdough breadcrumbs
1 tablespoon freshly squeezed
  lime juice
1–2 tablespoons coconut oil
4 large iceberg lettuce leaves

GREEN SAUCE
½ avocado
½ cup coconut milk, plus extra
  if needed
1 tablespoon freshly squeezed
  lime juice

To make the green sauce, blitz all the ingredients in a food processor or high-speed blender, adding more coconut milk if needed to make it a pouring consistency.

Place the chickpeas, garlic, chilli, cumin, turmeric, paprika, coriander, mint, breadcrumbs and lime juice in a food processor or high-speed blender and pulse until the mixture comes together (but do not puree). Add up to ½ cup of water if the mixture feels too dry to hold together. Transfer the mixture to a bowl and bring together with your hands, then cover and place in the fridge for 30 minutes.

Form heaped tablespoons of the falafel mixture into 24 small balls. Heat the coconut oil in a frying pan over medium heat and add the falafels. Cook for 5 minutes on each side or until browned and crisp. Drain on paper towel. Set half aside for tomorrow's lunch.

Serve the falafels in lettuce cups drizzled with the green sauce and with extra coriander.

Remember to use the good lettuce cups that you set aside when you made your smoothie this morning (see page 173).

HARISSA FISH *with* RADISH *and* ROAST CARROT SALAD

SERVES 2

Harissa is a Middle Eastern chilli-based spice blend. We're using the dry spice blend here but it can also be bought as a paste, which also works well. The roasted carrots are an excellent source of vitamin A and the peppery radish and bitter radicchio leaves are great for the liver. Delicious grilled peaches balance the bitterness. Feel free to add a scattering of feta or goat's cheese for a creamy finish.

- 1 bunch (8–12) baby heirloom carrots, tops trimmed
- 3 tablespoons extra virgin olive oil
- 2 firm white fish fillets (about 200 g in total)
- 1 tablespoon harissa spice blend
- 6 radishes, trimmed and quartered
- 1 peach, deseeded and cut into wedges
- 1 small head radicchio, leaves roughly torn
- 1 small handful of flat-leaf parsley leaves
- 2 tablespoons dukkah

DRESSING
- 1 tablespoon extra virgin olive oil
- 2 teaspoons balsamic vinegar

To make the dressing, combine the olive oil and vinegar in a bowl and mix well.

Preheat the oven to 180°C.

Place the carrots on a baking tray, drizzle with 1 tablespoon of the olive oil and bake for 20 minutes or until tender.

Meanwhile, coat the fish in the harissa and 1 tablespoon of the olive oil. Heat a frying pan over medium–high heat and cook the fish for 3–4 minutes each side until cooked through. When the fish is almost done, move it to one side of the pan, add the remaining olive oil and slightly caramelise the radish and peach pieces, about 1 minute.

Combine the carrots, radish, peach, radicchio, parsley and dukkah with the dressing, and serve with the fish.

OPEN LAMB BURGERS *with* COCONUT SAUCE

SERVES 2

Burgers are always a crowd favourite and they don't need to be excluded from a healthy diet! All we're doing here is halving the bread and focusing on nutritional goodness from the vegetables. I have used coconut yoghurt to make a tzatziki-style sauce but feel free to use unsweetened full-fat Greek yoghurt if you're okay with dairy. The harissa is a dry spice blend, but the paste is fine if that's what you have.

2 teaspoons ghee or butter
½ red onion, sliced
1 wholegrain bread roll, halved
1 handful of mixed lettuce
1 tomato, sliced
½ Lebanese cucumber, sliced
  into thin ribbons

LAMB BURGERS
250 g lamb mince
2 teaspoons harissa spice blend
½ onion, diced
1 clove garlic, crushed
1 handful of flat-leaf parsley
  leaves, finely chopped
1 organic egg

COCONUT SAUCE
3 tablespoons coconut yoghurt
  (or yoghurt of your choice)
1 tablespoon finely chopped
  mint
1 tablespoon freshly squeezed
  lemon juice
1 clove garlic, crushed
sea salt and freshly ground
  black pepper

To make the lamb burgers, combine the lamb, harissa, onion, garlic, parsley and egg and shape into two patties. Chill in the fridge for 30 minutes.

Heat 1 teaspoon of the ghee or butter in a frying pan over medium–high heat, add the onion and fry until starting to brown, 4–5 minutes. Remove the onion from the pan and set aside. Wipe the pan clean, add the remaining ghee or butter and cook the patties for 4–5 minutes on each side, until cooked through.

Meanwhile, to make the coconut sauce, combine all the ingredients in a bowl and mix well.

Toast the bun halves under the grill until lightly toasted, about 1–2 minutes. Spread some coconut sauce on top, add a lamb patty and top with the lettuce, tomato, cucumber and onion.

CHICKEN SKEWERS *with* CARROT, BEET *and* APPLE SALAD

SERVES 4

Tonight, we're making enough for tomorrow's lunch – and I think this salad tastes even better after the flavours have infused overnight! Beetroot is a fantastic blood tonic and the pigment that gives them their bright purple colour has been shown to have properties that may protect us against cancer. Kale is an exceptional source of chlorophyll, beta-carotene, and vitamins A and C. You can use metal or wooden skewers here but if you're using wooden ones soak them in water for 30 minutes first so they don't burn.

8 chicken thigh fillets (about 800 g in total), cut into thin strips
2 teaspoons ghee or butter
2 carrots, peeled and grated
1 beetroot, scrubbed, trimmed and grated
1 green apple, cut into matchsticks
4 large kale leaves, stalks discarded, shredded
½ cup mung beans
½ red onion, diced
1 small handful of mint leaves, chopped
1 small handful of flat-leaf parsley leaves, chopped
3 tablespoons currants
lemon wedges, to serve

DRESSING
2 tablespoons extra virgin olive oil
1 tablespoon freshly squeezed lemon juice
1 teaspoon honey
1 teaspoon dijon mustard
sea salt and freshly ground black pepper

To make the dressing, combine all the ingredients in a bowl and mix well.

Thread the chicken onto 8 skewers. Preheat a char-grill pan and add the ghee or butter. Grill the chicken for 4–5 minutes on each side until cooked through.

Meanwhile, combine the carrot, beetroot, apple, kale, mung beans, onion, mint, parsley and currants, then pour over the dressing.

Serve the salad with two chicken skewers each, with lemon wedges alongside for squeezing over.

MUSSEL SPAGHETTI
with TOMATOES *and* GARLIC

SERVES 2

Mussels are a sustainable seafood option and low in mercury, something we want to avoid. A great protein source, they also contain plenty of selenium and omega-3 fats and go perfectly with this tomato-based pasta dish. Ask your fishmonger to debeard and clean them for you. When the mussels are cooked, the shell will naturally open to reveal the pearl–silver meat inside. Any that don't open can be thrown away.

250 g wholegrain spaghetti
1 tablespoon extra virgin olive oil, plus extra for drizzling
2 cloves garlic, crushed
½ long red chilli, finely sliced and deseeded if you like
1½ cups cherry tomatoes
1 heaped tablespoon tomato paste
500 g mussels, scrubbed and debearded
2 handfuls of kale leaves, stalks discarded, finely chopped
1 handful of flat-leaf parsley leaves

Bring a large saucepan of water with a pinch of salt to the boil and cook the spaghetti for 13 minutes or until al dente.

Meanwhile, heat the olive oil in a wok over low–medium heat and cook the garlic and chilli for 1 minute. Add the tomatoes and tomato paste and cook for another 2–3 minutes. Add the mussels to the wok, then place the lid on and steam the mussels until they have opened and the tomatoes have collapsed, about 5 minutes (discard any mussels that don't open).

Drain the spaghetti, reserving 2 tablespoons of the cooking liquid, then return to the saucepan. Stir through the kale and a drizzle of olive oil, then pour over the mussels and tomato. Add the parsley, mix well and serve.

MUSTARD PORK *with* ROAST PEAR SALAD

SERVES 2

Roasting fruit is a delicious way to add flavour to your meals. The protein in the pork, healthy fats in the olive oil and the ground cinnamon all work to help stabilise blood-sugar levels.

1 pear, cored and cut into
  12 wedges
½ sweet potato, peeled and cut
  into thick matchsticks
1 teaspoon ground cinnamon
1 tablespoon maple syrup
2 teaspoons dijon mustard
2 teaspoons extra virgin olive
  oil, plus extra for drizzling
sea salt and freshly ground
  black pepper
2 × 200 g pork cutlets
2 handfuls of rocket
4 radishes, trimmed and shaved
  into thin rounds
2 tablespoons raw pistachio
  kernels, roughly chopped
juice of ½ lemon

Preheat the oven to 180°C and line a baking tray with baking paper.

Lay the pear wedges on one half of the prepared tray and the sweet potato on the other half. Sprinkle the cinnamon over the pears and toss. Roast the pears and sweet potato for 15–20 minutes until tender.

Meanwhile, combine the maple syrup, mustard, olive oil and salt and pepper. Rub over the pork cutlets. Cook the pork in a frying pan over medium–high heat for 4–5 minutes on each side until cooked through. Remove from the heat, cover with foil and rest for 5 minutes.

Combine the rocket, radish and pistachios with the roast pear and sweet potato. Squeeze over the lemon juice and drizzle with olive oil. Serve with the pork cutlets.

MEXICAN BEEF *with* SALSA

SERVES 2

This dish is similar to a chilli con carne, but here we are serving it with a lively salsa instead of rice. The raw cacao powder is extremely high in antioxidants and is a great source of magnesium. It has a bitter chocolate taste, which works here to give a richer flavour to the mince.

2 tablespoons ghee or butter
½ onion, diced
1 clove garlic, crushed
1 small red chilli, chopped and deseeded if you like
250 g beef mince
2 teaspoons smoked paprika
1 teaspoon ground cumin
1 teaspoon ground coriander
2 teaspoons raw cacao powder
1 heaped tablespoon tomato paste
1 small sweet potato, peeled and grated
1 corn cob, husk removed and kernels sliced off
1 small red capsicum, deseeded and diced
1 small green capsicum, deseeded and diced
½ cup cherry tomatoes, quartered
1 handful of coriander leaves
½ avocado, diced
juice of ½ lime
lime wedges, to serve

Heat the ghee or butter in a frying pan over medium heat and saute the onion for 2 minutes. Add the garlic and chilli and saute for another minute, then add the mince. Brown for 2 minutes, breaking it up with a wooden spoon, then add the paprika, cumin, ground coriander and cacao powder. Stir for 10 seconds, then add the tomato paste, sweet potato, corn and 2 tablespoons of water and cook for 3–4 minutes, then remove from the heat.

Meanwhile, combine the capsicums, tomatoes, coriander leaves, avocado and lime juice and gently mix together.

Serve the Mexican beef with the salsa and lime wedges.

SPICED SALMON *with* GRILLED WATERMELON

SERVES 2

This is a surprisingly delicious combination of juicy flavours! The extra green pea puree will keep in the fridge for up to a week and is delicious with grilled meats.

2 salmon fillets (about
    200–250 g in total)
1 teaspoon ghee or butter
2 slices watermelon,
    about 2 cm thick
1 Lebanese cucumber, diced
6 coriander leaves
1 handful of mint leaves
lime wedges, to serve

TANDOORI PASTE MARINADE

50 g tandoori paste
3 tablespoons organic,
    full-fat coconut cream
2½ tablespoons garam masala
pinch of sea salt
juice of ½ lemon
2.5 cm piece of ginger, peeled
    and grated
2 cloves garlic, crushed
1 tablespoon chopped
    coriander leaves

GREEN PEA PUREE

1 tablespoon coconut oil
1 onion, chopped
2 teaspoons fennel seeds,
    ground
50 g raw cashew nuts
2 long green chillies,
    finely chopped
200 ml organic, full-fat
    coconut cream
500 g frozen peas
1 handful of coriander leaves

To make the tandoori paste marinade, combine all the ingredients in a high-speed blender and blend to make a paste.

Score the skin of the salmon and then rub the paste all over. Cover and place in the fridge for 3 hours to marinate.

Preheat the oven to 180°C and line a baking tray with baking paper.

To make the green pea puree, heat the coconut oil in a frying pan over medium heat and gently fry the onion and fennel seeds until the onion is translucent. Add the cashew nuts, chilli and coconut cream and bring to a simmer. Cook for 5 minutes, then add the peas and coriander, and cook for a further 2 minutes. Remove from the heat and carefully transfer to a food processor or high-speed blender and blitz to combine. Pass through a fine sieve and set aside, covered to keep warm.

Heat the ghee or butter in a frying pan over medium heat and fry the salmon, skin-side down, until browned, about 2 minutes. Place on the prepared tray and bake in the oven until cooked to your liking, about 10 minutes.

Wipe the frying pan clean and cook the watermelon over medium–high heat for 2–3 minutes on each side.

To make the salad, combine the cucumber and coriander. Spread some green pea puree on serving plates. Place the watermelon on the green pea puree and top with the salmon. Garnish with mint and serve with the salad and lime wedges.

INDIAN SPICED CHICKEN *with* SESAME *and* SWEET POTATO MASH

SERVES 2

I'm sure you've realised by now how much I love spicy food! This dish takes meal prep up a notch with the awesome aromatics found in Indian cooking, while still being full of clean protein and filling low-GI carbs. Plus, these spices don't just bring incredible flavour, they also have serious nutritional powers – they are anti-ageing, anti-inflammatory, immune-boosting, full of antioxidants and great for our digestion.

400 g chicken breast, sliced into strips about 2 cm thick and 6 cm long
1 tablespoon organic, full-fat coconut cream
sea salt
500 g orange sweet potato, peeled and chopped into about eight cubes
1 head broccoli, cut into florets, stalks trimmed and diced
1 tablespoon coconut oil
1 tablespoon sesame seeds

INDIAN SPICE MIX
½ teaspoon curry powder
½ teaspoon ground cumin
½ teaspoon ground turmeric
½ teaspoon ground coriander
¼ teaspoon ground ginger

To make the Indian spice mix, combine all the ingredients in a bowl and mix well.

Place the chicken in a shallow bowl with the spice mix, coconut cream and ½ teaspoon of salt. Cover and place in the fridge to marinate while you make the sweet potato mash.

Place the sweet potato in a saucepan with a pinch of salt and cover with water. Bring to the boil and cook for about 10 minutes until the sweet potato is soft when pricked with a fork.

Meanwhile, bring ½ cup of water to the boil in a small saucepan. If you have a steamer, place the steamer on top and add the broccoli; if not you can place the broccoli directly into the water. Steam for 5 minutes until the broccoli is just tender but still vibrant green.

Melt the coconut oil in a large frying pan over medium–high heat, then add the marinated chicken and cook for about 2 minutes on each side.

Mash the sweet potato using a fork, then spoon it onto two plates and season with salt and pepper. Arrange the chicken alongside, sprinkle with the sesame seeds and serve with the broccoli.

SPICED LAMB *with* QUINOA, BEETROOT HUMMUS *and* GREENS

SERVES 2

Channel your inner master chef and paint your plate with the vibrant colours of beetroot hummus, all while enjoying the antioxidant and anti-inflammatory support of these purple powers. If you're opting for store-bought hummus, check the label and avoid any preservatives or ingredients you can't pronounce!

I cup quinoa
2 teaspoons ground cumin
2 teaspoons ground coriander
I teaspoon chilli powder
¼ teaspoon smoked paprika
sea salt and freshly ground
   black pepper
350 g lamb backstrap
I tablespoon extra virgin
   olive oil
2 tablespoons slivered almonds
I bunch broccolini, trimmed

BEETROOT HUMMUS

450 g tinned beetroot, drained
I × 400 g tin chickpeas, drained
   and rinsed
finely grated zest and juice
   of 2 lemons
2 cloves garlic, crushed
I tablespoon tahini
pinch of sea salt
2 tablespoons extra virgin
   olive oil

To make the beetroot hummus, place all the ingredients in a food processor or high-speed blender and blend until well combined, adding enough water to reach a smooth consistency, if necessary. This will keep in the fridge for up to a week and is delicious with vegetable sticks or as an addition to your eggs on toast.

Rinse the quinoa well and place it in a saucepan with 2 cups of water. Bring to the boil, then reduce the heat to low and simmer until the water has been absorbed and the quinoa 'tails' appear, about 12–15 minutes. Remove from the heat and set aside, with the lid on, for 5 minutes, then fluff with a fork.

While the quinoa is cooking, combine the spices, salt and pepper. Rub the mix over the lamb with the olive oil.

Heat a non-stick frying pan over medium–high heat and fry the lamb for 3 minutes on each side for medium–rare for a thin backstrap (thicker pieces will need 4 minutes on each side for the same result). Remove from the heat and allow to rest for 3 minutes before slicing.

Wipe the pan clean and toast the almonds over medium heat for 2 minutes or until golden brown.

Set a steamer over a saucepan of simmering water. Place the broccolini in the steamer and lightly steam until just tender, about 5 minutes, then rinse under cold water.

Smear 2 tablespoons of beetroot hummus across each plate, spoon the quinoa on top and scatter over the toasted almonds. Arrange the broccolini on top and finish with the sliced lamb.

If you're pressed for time, you can swap out the homemade beetroot hummus for store-bought – choose a variety without extra sugar or added preservatives.

SWEET POTATO CHICKEN 'NACHOS' (SEE PAGE 306)

MEXICAN SPICED CHICKEN WITH SWEET POTATO (SEE PAGE 303)

CHICKEN BURRITO BOWL (SEE PAGE 302)

CHICKEN BURRITO BOWL

SERVES 2

I've been lucky enough to have enjoyed some amazing trips to Mexico and I love incorporating the flavours into my cooking. This homemade burrito bowl ensures you're steering clear of the hidden sugars and preservatives often found in the takeaway version. Brown rice is a nurturing source of energy, thanks to the B vitamins it contains. Corn provides a hit of vitamin C and can help to protect against eye disease.

¾ cup brown rice
1 corn cob, husk removed
400 g chicken thigh fillets
2 tablespoons coconut oil
2 cups baby spinach
1 × 400 g tin red kidney beans, drained and rinsed
½ long (telegraph) cucumber, chopped into 1 cm cubes
1 tomato, chopped into 1 cm cubes
1 avocado, halved
extra virgin olive oil, for drizzling
lime wedges, to serve

SPICE MIX
½ teaspoon chilli powder
½ teaspoon dried oregano
1 teaspoon smoked paprika
1 teaspoon ground cumin
pinch of garlic powder
pinch of onion powder
sea salt and freshly ground black pepper

Place the rice in a saucepan with 1½ cups of water and a pinch of salt. Bring to the boil, then reduce the heat to low, cover and simmer for 40 minutes. Check whether most of the water has been absorbed and the rice is tender (drain any excess water, or add a bit more and simmer for another 5 minutes if no excess water). Remove from the heat and allow to cool.

Meanwhile, place the corn in another saucepan with enough water to cover. Add a pinch of salt and bring to the boil. Allow to boil for 5–7 minutes. Remove from the heat, drain and rinse under cold water. Set aside to cool, then slice off the kernels.

While the rice and corn are cooking, make the spice mix by combining all the ingredients in a small dish. Rub the chicken with 1 tablespoon of the coconut oil, then coat it in the spice mix.

Melt the remaining coconut oil in a large frying pan over medium heat. Add the chicken and cook for 8 minutes or until cooked through, turning halfway. Remove from the pan and leave to cool for 5 minutes. Chop the chicken into strips.

Divide the rice between two bowls and add the spinach. Top with the chicken, corn, kidney beans, cucumber, tomato and avocado. Drizzle over the olive oil and serve with lime wedges.

MEXICAN SPICED CHICKEN *with* SWEET POTATO

SERVES 2

2 tablespoons extra virgin
  olive oil
juice of 1½ limes
1 tablespoon chopped
  coriander leaves, plus a few
  extra leaves for the mashed
  avocado
400 g chicken breast
1 large sweet potato, peeled
  and chopped
1 tablespoon coconut oil
6 baby corn
½ avocado
sea salt and freshly ground
  black pepper
10 baby cos lettuce leaves
6 cherry tomatoes, halved
lime wedges, for serving

MEXICAN SPICE MIX

1 tablespoon cumin seeds
1 tablespoon chilli powder
1 tablespoon paprika
1 tablespoon cayenne pepper
1 tablespoon dried oregano
2 teaspoons ground coriander
2 teaspoons garlic powder

MEXICAN DRESSING

1 tablespoon extra virgin
  olive oil
juice of 1 lime
pinch of minced garlic
1 handful of coriander leaves
1 teaspoon honey

To make the Mexican spice mix, combine all the ingredients. This makes 6 tablespoons; it will keep sealed in an airtight container for up to a month.

Combine 2 tablespoons of the Mexican spice mix with 1 tablespoon of the olive oil, juice of ½ lime and the chopped coriander to make a paste. Coat the chicken breast with the paste, then cover and place in the fridge to marinate for 4 hours or overnight.

Preheat the oven to 200°C and line a baking tray with baking paper.

Place the sweet potato on the prepared tray and drizzle with the remaining olive oil. Roast for 20–30 minutes, tossing halfway, until soft and golden.

Melt the coconut oil in a large frying pan over medium heat. Add the chicken and cook for 8 minutes or until cooked through, turning halfway. Add the corn and fry for 5 minutes or until starting to brown. Remove the chicken from the pan and leave to cool for 5 minutes before slicing.

While the chicken cools, make the dressing by shaking all the ingredients in a screw-top jar.

Mash the avocado and combine with the remaining lime juice and a few coriander leaves, then season with salt and pepper.

Arrange the lettuce leaves on a platter and place the corn, tomatoes, sweet potato and chicken on top. Serve drizzled with the dressing, with the mashed avocado and lime wedges on the side.

MUM'S FAMOUS CHICKEN DRUMSTICKS

SERVES 4

This is my mum's seriously epic take on Colonel Sanders. It's not only easy to make, there's zero oil involved, yet the recipe is just as juicy as the fried alternative. This seasoning also works brilliantly on wings – the perfect addition to any summer barbecue! Choose a burrito mix with no added sugar and preservatives, or even better use the spice mix from the Mexican Spiced Chicken with Sweet Potato on page 303.

10–12 chicken drumsticks
2 organic eggs
1¼ cups cornflake crumbs
1 × 40 g sachet of burrito mix

SIMPLE COLESLAW
1 green apple
juice of 1 lemon
2 carrots, peeled and sliced
    into ribbons using a vegetable
    peeler, or spiralised
    (see page 253)
1½ cups shredded red cabbage
6 sprigs mint, leaves picked
extra virgin olive oil,
    for drizzling

Rinse and pat the chicken dry and set aside. In a deep bowl, whisk the eggs together. In a separate bowl, combine the cornflake crumbs and burrito mix, and transfer to a plate. Place a wire oven rack alongside.

Dip the drumsticks one at a time into the egg and roll in the crumb and burrito mix to coat, then transfer to the wire rack. Transfer to the fridge for 30 minutes to set.

Preheat the oven to 200°C.

Fill a baking dish or roasting tin with 1 cm of water and place the wire rack of drumsticks on top, ensuring the water does not touch the chicken. Bake for 40 minutes or until the coating is browned and crispy.

While the chicken is baking, prepare your slaw. Slice the apple into matchsticks and place in a salad bowl. Squeeze over the lemon juice and toss to coat (this will prevent the apple from browning). Toss the carrot and cabbage through the apple and tear the mint leaves over. Finish with a drizzle of olive oil, then serve.

SWEET POTATO CHICKEN 'NACHOS'

SERVES 2

The Mexican fiesta continues! Swapping corn chips for sweet potato fills us up with low-GI fuel, plus we're enjoying lean protein from the beans and chicken, vitamin-C vibes from the corn and tomatoes, and liver support from our coriander garnish.

I large orange sweet potato, peeled and sliced into 5 mm rounds
sea salt and freshly ground black pepper
I corn cob, husk removed
I tablespoon coconut oil
400 g chicken thigh fillets, halved
I avocado
I tablespoon chopped coriander leaves, plus extra leaves to garnish
juice of ½ lime
½ × 400 g tin black beans, drained and rinsed
I cup cherry tomatoes, quartered

Preheat the oven to 200°C and line a baking tray with baking paper.

Season the sweet potato with salt and pepper and place on the prepared tray. Roast for 30 minutes or until crispy.

Meanwhile, place the corn cob in a saucepan and cover with boiling water and a pinch of salt. Cook for 4–7 minutes, then remove from the pan and rinse under cold water. Set aside to cool for 5 minutes, then carefully slice off the kernels.

Heat the coconut oil in a frying pan over medium–high heat. Season the chicken with salt and pepper, add to the pan and fry for 5 minutes, then turn over and fry for a further 3 minutes or until cooked through. Remove from the heat and leave to cool before shredding with a fork.

In a bowl, smash the avocado with a generous seasoning of salt and pepper, the chopped coriander and lime juice.

Take the sweet potato chips out of the oven and lay them out on a platter. Cover with the beans, shredded chicken, tomatoes and corn. Dollop the avocado smash on top and scatter with the extra coriander leaves.

If you'd like to add cheese, use half an avocado instead of a whole one and scatter 3 tablespoons of grated cheddar over the top to serve.

COUNTRY BEEF HOTPOT

SERVES 2

Don't worry about spending hours chopping your veg for this dish – just throw them in and watch the magic happen! With protein from the beef to build lean muscle, carbohydrates and vitamin C from the carrots for energy and immunity, vitamin D from the mushrooms for healthy bones, and the superpowers of spinach, this dish is a nutritional hug for your whole body.

2 tablespoons extra virgin olive oil
1 onion, sliced into thin wedges
2 cloves garlic, crushed
3 sprigs thyme, leaves picked
sea salt and freshly ground black pepper
250 g (about 8–10) button mushrooms, stems removed
4 Dutch carrots, trimmed
300–350 g beef fillet, such as sirloin or scotch, sliced into strips 1 cm wide and 3 cm long
½ cup vegetable stock
3 tablespoons organic, full-fat coconut milk
2 cups baby spinach
1 sprig flat-leaf parsley, leaves chopped

Heat 1 tablespoon of the olive oil in a large saucepan over low–medium heat and gently fry the onion and garlic for 2–3 minutes to soften. Scatter over the thyme and season with salt and pepper, then add the mushrooms and carrots and toss through. Cook for 5–6 minutes, stirring once or twice. Remove the vegetables from the pan and set aside.

Return the pan to medium heat, add the remaining olive oil and sear the beef for 1–2 minutes, until browned all over. Be careful not to overcook as it can become tough. Add the stock, then return the vegetables to the pan and toss to combine. Add the coconut milk and stir to warm through.

Remove the pan from the heat and stir the spinach leaves through just before serving. Spoon into bowls and top with the parsley.

FIERY RED LAMB CURRY

SERVES 2

This is a deliciously warming, flavour-packed curry that won't leave you in a food coma! Perfect for a winter weekend spent around the house, it's super-quick to prepare, then you can pop it in the oven and sit back and relax while your house fills with the incredible aromas. It's also easily doubled to prep for the week ahead. I've used red rice in this recipe but you can substitute white or brown if you prefer.

1 tablespoon coconut oil
1 teaspoon brown
   mustard seeds
350 g diced lamb leg or
   shoulder
½ teaspoon ground turmeric
2 teaspoons madras
   curry powder
½ teaspoon chilli powder
   (optional, if you like it hot!)
1 onion, sliced
2 cloves garlic, crushed
2.5 cm piece of ginger, peeled
   and grated
10 fresh curry leaves
1 × 400 g tin crushed tomatoes
sea salt and freshly ground
   black pepper
1 × 270 g tin organic,
   full-fat coconut milk
1 cup red rice
2 large handfuls of baby spinach
4 sprigs coriander or flat-leaf
   parsley

Preheat the oven to 150°C.

Heat the coconut oil in a flameproof casserole dish over medium heat. Add the mustard seeds and cook, stirring, for 1 minute or until the seeds start to pop. Add the lamb, turmeric, curry powder and chilli powder, if using, and cook, stirring, for 2–3 minutes or until the lamb is browned all over. Add the onion, garlic, ginger and curry leaves and stir to combine. Reduce the heat slightly and add the tomatoes and ½ cup of water. Season with salt and pepper. Cover with the lid and place in the oven for 2½ hours.

Remove from the oven and return to the stovetop over medium heat. Stir through the coconut milk and simmer to thicken while you prepare the rice.

Rinse your rice thoroughly, then place it in a saucepan with 3 cups of water and a pinch of salt. Cover and bring to the boil. Reduce the heat and simmer for 30 minutes or until the rice has softened and the water has been absorbed.

Place a handful of spinach leaves in the bottom of each bowl and spoon over the rice and curry. Garnish with herbs to serve.

Madras curry is a slightly spicier variation on normal curry powder.

Rice alternative

For a quicker alternative to rice, microwave poppadums two at a time for 1 minute on high. The light and crispy texture is a nice contrast and a great way to scoop up the creamy curry sauce.

Snacks and Desserts

BANANA NICE CREAM *with* CHOC GRANOLA

SERVES 2

Two-ingredient ice-cream? Yes, please! Natural, creamy, delicious and so easy! Bonus points for the potassium boost from the bananas and the immune-boosting vitamin E in the almond milk, which promotes healthy skin. Serve this with my choc granola topping, or simply enjoy it on its own.

3 frozen peeled bananas
3 tablespoons almond milk
(unsweetened)

CHOC GRANOLA
2 tablespoons coconut oil
½ cup rolled oats
½ cup chopped mixed nuts
(I like almonds and cashews)
1 tablespoon honey
1 tablespoon raw cacao powder

Blend the bananas and almond milk together in a food processer or high-speed blender until smooth and creamy. Place in the freezer until you are ready to serve.

To make the choc granola, melt 1½ tablespoons of the coconut oil in a large saucepan over low heat, about 2 minutes (or melt it in the microwave for 10 seconds). Pour the melted coconut oil into a bowl with all the other granola ingredients and mix together.

Add the remaining coconut oil to the pan along with the granola mixture. Toast over medium–high heat for 3–5 minutes until golden brown, stirring to ensure it doesn't burn, then remove from the heat. Sprinkle the granola over the nice cream and serve.

Old bananas?

Don't throw away your bananas when they start to get brown spots! Simply remove the skins, slice into quarters, seal in a zip-lock bag, and place in the freezer. This makes them much easier to add to recipes like this!

CHOC NUT BANANA ICE POPS

MAKES 6

If you don't have a blender, you don't have to miss out on the frozen goodness! These ice pops are the perfect dessert or afternoon treat. They feature potassium, magnesium, antioxidants, essential nutrients and healthy fats — as if we needed any more excuses.

2 large or 3 small frozen peeled bananas, cut into thirds or halves (see page 313)
70 g dark chocolate (at least 60 per cent cocoa), chopped
½ cup mixed nuts (almonds, peanuts and cashews are my faves here), finely chopped

Leave the frozen bananas to thaw for a few minutes, then carefully insert an ice-cream stick into each one to make baby popsicles.

Place 1 cup of water in a saucepan and bring to a gentle simmer. Place the chocolate in a heatproof bowl set on top of the saucepan, ensuring that the water below does not touch the bowl. Stir the chocolate gently for about 5 minutes, or until it has melted. Remove the bowl from the heat and set aside for a few minutes, to allow the chocolate to thicken.

Lay out the chopped nuts on a plate. Line a baking tray with baking paper and place it alongside. Dip one banana pop at a time into the bowl of melted chocolate, tilting the bowl if necessary to coat all sides. While the chocolate is still wet, roll the banana pop on the plate of nuts. Hold it upright for a few moments, rotating to avoid any drips, then place it on the baking tray. Repeat the process for the remaining pops.

Place the chocolate-covered banana pops in the freezer for at least 30 minutes to set. Keep stored in the freezer until you are ready to eat!

WATERMELON *and* RASPBERRY SORBET

MAKES ABOUT 1 LITRE

An awesome tangy addition to your homemade ice-cream parlour! The double-blend helps to break down the slushy texture for a smoother end result.

700 g watermelon, rind removed
1 × 125 g punnet raspberries
juice of ½ lime

Blend all the ingredients in a food processor or high-speed blender for 2–3 minutes or until completely liquefied. Transfer into a container and place in the freezer for 1 hour.

Remove from the freezer and transfer the mixture to the food processor. Blend for 1 minute, then return to the freezer for 3–4 hours or until ready to serve.

MANGO *and* COCONUT GELATO

SERVES 4

A deliciously cool and creamy treat for those hot summer days! Buy up your mangoes while they're in season, peel and slice, then store in the freezer and the feelings of summer will never be far away.

1 banana, peeled and chopped
2 mangoes, peeled, deseeded and chopped
½ cup coconut yoghurt (or yoghurt of your choice)

Place the banana and mango pieces in the freezer for 2–3 hours or until frozen.

Remove from the freezer and place in a food processor with the coconut yoghurt. Blend until smooth and creamy.

Serve or return to the freezer until you are ready to eat!

WATERMELON PIZZA

SERVES 8

The possibilities are endless here! Play around with your favourite summer fruits – peaches, nectarines, mangoes, kiwi fruit and blackberries are all delicious. Use any leftover watermelon to make a refreshing sorbet (see page 317).

1 whole watermelon
1 cup coconut yoghurt (or yoghurt of your choice)
1 × 125 g punnet raspberries or 1 × 250 g punnet strawberries
1 × 125 g punnet blueberries
4 sprigs mint, leaves picked
1 passionfruit (optional)

Cut a 2.5 cm thick slice out of the watermelon and lay it flat. Cut the slice into 6–8 pieces, depending on its size.

Spread the yoghurt from the tip of each watermelon piece almost to the edges, leaving a few centimetres of pink showing.

Scatter the berries and mint leaves over the top, and drizzle with passionfruit, if using.

CASHEW, RASPBERRY
and COCONUT CHOCOLATE BARK

MAKES A 20 CM × 20 CM SHEET

This chocolate brittle will not only satisfy any sweet cravings but is also full of magnesium and iron! Cocoa has been shown to give us a similar buzz of endorphins like we get after an awesome training session. Perfect for a post-dinner treat or for a high-energy snack.

3 tablespoons coconut oil
50 g dark chocolate
   (at least 60 per cent cocoa),
   roughly chopped
1 tablespoon maple syrup
   or honey
3 tablespoons raw cacao
   powder
½ teaspoon pure vanilla extract
3 tablespoons chopped cashews
3 tablespoons chopped
   raspberries
1 tablespoon coconut flakes

Melt the coconut oil in a small saucepan over medium heat. Reduce the heat to low and add the chocolate, maple syrup or honey and cacao powder. Melt, stirring frequently, for 5–6 minutes until smooth. Remove from the heat and stir in the vanilla, then leave to cool for 10 minutes to allow the chocolate to thicken.

Line a baking tray (about 20 cm × 20 cm) with baking paper and gently pour over the chocolate so it forms a sheet about 5 mm thick.

Sprinkle over the cashews, raspberries and coconut flakes. Place in the freezer for at least 2 hours to harden.

When ready to serve, remove from the freezer, break into shards and enjoy! Keep the remaining bark stored in the freezer.

Check your tray fits in the freezer before you pour the chocolate in!

Mix it up!

Instead of cashews, raspberries and coconut flakes, mix it up with different combinations of your favourite toppings! Here are some ideas:

- Toasted slivered almonds
- Chopped raw pistachio kernels
- Chopped unsalted peanuts
- Glazed ginger
- Sea salt
- Chilli flakes
- Freeze-dried strawberries
- Dried cranberries
- Coffee beans

Show me your creations on Instagram with #summerfitz

Snacks and Desserts

COOKIE DOUGH VANILLA PROTEIN BUTTONS

MAKES 9 SMALL BUTTONS

These protein-packed buttons are a perfect addition to your bag on a weekend hike or beach adventure, or a post-workout snack. The oats and protein powder combined will keep you powering through! Protein is not only great for long-lasting energy, but it's essential for healthy skin, hair and nails.

½ cup rolled oats
3 tablespoons vanilla pea protein powder (or your favourite flavour)
3 tablespoons melted coconut oil
1 tablespoon nut butter (I like peanut or almond here)
1 tablespoon honey
3 tablespoons dark chocolate chips (at least 60 per cent cocoa)

In a food processer, blend the oats until they reach a flour-like consistency, then add the protein powder, coconut oil, nut butter, honey and 2 tablespoons of the dark chocolate chips. Blend to form a dough.

Line a plate or baking tray with baking paper. Using a tablespoon of mixture at a time, roll into 3 cm balls and place on the tray, leaving a few centimetres around each one to allow for spreading. Using your palm, gently flatten each ball so it forms a button. Press the remaining chocolate chips into the top of the buttons.

Place the buttons in the fridge for at least 30 minutes to harden. Store in the fridge for up to a week, if they last that long!

BLUEBERRY MUFFINS

MAKES 12

Steer clear of store-bought cakes and muffins and their sneaky hidden sugars with this quick, easy and incredibly fluffy alternative. I love loading up the berries for a juicy hit of antioxidants. These muffins are unbeatable straight from the oven but will keep for 2–3 days in an airtight container.

½ cup macadamia oil, plus extra for greasing
3 cups almond meal
1 tablespoon baking powder
½ teaspoon ground cinnamon, plus extra for dusting
3 tablespoons maple syrup
finely grated zest of 1 lemon
3 organic eggs
¾ cup coconut yoghurt (or yoghurt of your choice)
1 cup frozen or fresh blueberries

Preheat the oven to 200°C and grease and/or line a 12-hole ⅓ cup capacity muffin tray.

Combine all the ingredients except the blueberries in a bowl and stir well to combine. Gently fold through the blueberries. Spoon the mixture into the prepared muffin holes and dust the tops with cinnamon.

Bake for 15 minutes or until the muffins spring back to the touch.

Cool in the tin for 5 minutes before transferring to a wire rack.

Muffin liners

To make paper liners for your muffins, cut 12 squares of baking paper measuring 12 cm × 12 cm. Find a jar or tin the same size as the base of your muffin holes and press the paper squares over it to create the shape you need. Then pop the liners into the muffin holes, and spoon the mixture in! Don't worry if some drops of batter land on the edges – it shows you've gone to the effort to make the muffins yourself, and is also really easy to remove when they come out of the oven :)

SALTED DATE CARAMEL SLICE

MAKES 25

This no-bake slice is the ultimate indulgent treat! With all natural sugars and healthy fats, it's also a great alternative to anything out of a packet.

BASE
⅔ cup almond meal
⅔ cup desiccated coconut
5 medjool dates, pitted
60 g raw almonds
pinch of sea salt
⅓ cup coconut oil, melted

FILLING
1½ cups raw cashews
1 cup boiling water, plus
    extra for soaking
300 g medjool dates, pitted
1 tablespoon maple syrup
75 g coconut oil, melted
1 teaspoon pure vanilla extract
pinch of sea salt

TOPPING
⅓ cup raw cacao powder
½ cup coconut oil, melted
1 tablespoon maple syrup
½ teaspoon pure vanilla extract

Line a 20 cm × 20 cm cake tin with baking paper.

For the filling, place the cashews in a bowl and cover with boiling water. Set aside to soak while you prepare the base.

To make the base, place all the ingredients except the coconut oil in a food processor and blend until you reach a sandy consistency, about 1 minute. Remove the bowl from the food processor and pour over the coconut oil, then use a spoon or your hands to combine. Press the base firmly into the bottom of your tin, making sure there are no gaps. Place in the freezer while you prepare the filling.

Drain the cashews and place in a small saucepan with the dates and boiling water. Bring to the boil, then reduce the heat and simmer, stirring constantly, for about 5 minutes or until all the water has evaporated and the dates are soft. Transfer the dates and cashews to the cleaned food processor, add all the other filling ingredients and blitz for 4–5 minutes, scraping down the edges as needed, until smooth and creamy. Allow the filling to cool for 5 minutes before spreading evenly over the base. Return to the freezer.

To make the topping, combine all the ingredients and mix well. Allow to cool and thicken for 10 minutes, then pour over the filling.

Return the slice to the freezer for 1 hour or the fridge for 3–4 hours to set. Use a hot, sharp knife to cut the slices into 4 cm squares. It will keep in the freezer for 1 week – if you can make it last that long!

INDEX

Working with an epic team is so much fun!

And that's a wrap! Our incredible crew.

Sharing a love of avocado toast with guru nutritionist, Steph.

Thank You!

I am so stoked to connect with you :-) It means a lot to me for you to pick up this book and allow me to join you on this awesome journey to be your best healthy self. Connecting our All Australian Beach Body community and watching it grow is the most incredible experience and I am continually inspired by your energy, your stories and your passion for health.

To the awesome team who have made this book possible – thank you! The unbelievably talented **Steph Wearne**, thank you for the expertise and creativity you have brought to this project. I love sharing that vision and bringing it to life with you.

To my Fitzgibbons International crew – Mike, Lara, Lucas, Jayne, Jon, Andy, Bruna, Claire and Jes, thank you for all your tireless hard work on this and all our projects. To **Gretchen Walker** – an extra special thank you for making everything we work on so much fun. Your determination, work ethic and enthusiasm was incredible in bringing this book to life. I am so proud of our team and everything we achieve together.

The amazing team at Pan Macmillan – Ingrid, Danielle, Megan, Susie, Ariane, Melody, Vanessa, Tracey, Kirby, Jeremy, Josh, Paulie and Rob – thank you for your inspiring passion, creativity, expertise and energy on this project.

Finally, to my source of inspiration – **my mum and dad** – thank you for giving me every opportunity, teaching me your incredible values, supporting me through highs and lows, and making this wild ride so much fun.

First published 2018 in Macmillan
by Pan Macmillan Australia Pty Limited
1 Market Street, Sydney, New South Wales
Australia 2000

A CIP catalogue record for this book is available from the National Library of Australia: http://catalogue.nla.gov.au

Design by Kirby Armstrong
Photography by Rob Palmer (with additional photography by Jeremy Simons and Lucas Townsend)
Prop and food styling by Vanessa Austen
Editing by Susie Ashworth
Recipe editing by Ariane Durkin
4-week meal plan and recipes developed with nutritionist Steph Wearne from Body Good Food.
Additional recipes by Gretchen Walker and Tasha Meyes
Typesetting by Post Pre-press Group, Brisbane
Index by Frances Paterson
Colour reproduction by Splitting Image Colour Studio
Printed and bound in China by Imago Printing International Limited

10 9 8 7 6 5 4 3 2 1

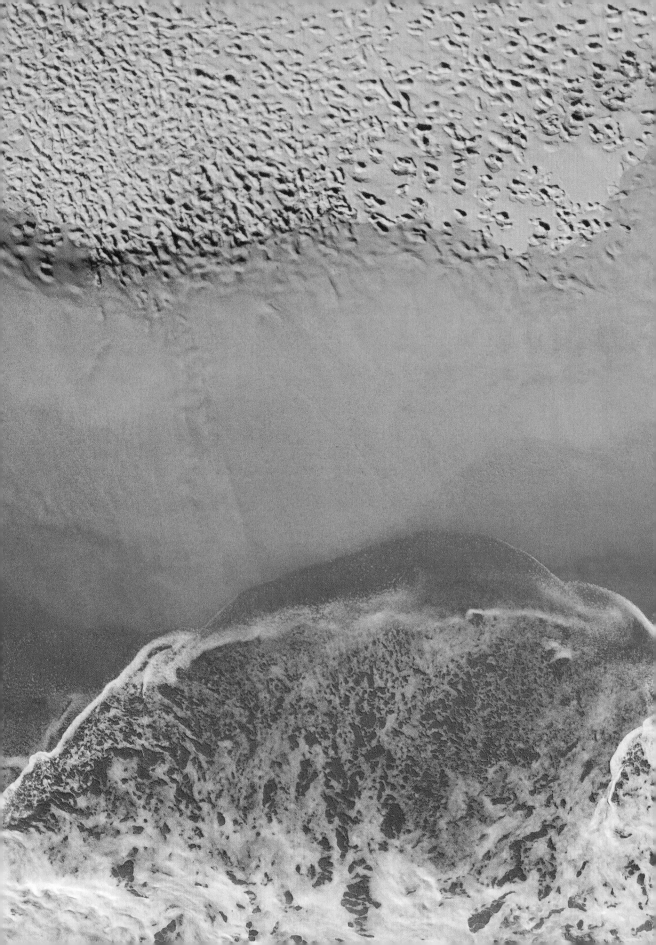